The Silk Press

Grosvenor House
45 The Downs Altrincham
Cheshire WA14 2QG
Tel. 0161 9294884 or 0161 9280333
Fax. 070707 39898

© Matthew Hyde 1999
ISBN 1 902685 04 0

Cover illustrations from the sketchbook of H T Gaddum
courtesy Anthony Gaddum

Cover design, layout and typesetting
Christine Pemberton

Printed by Redwood Books,
Trowbridge,
Wiltshire BA14 8RN

THE VILLAS
OF ALDERLEY EDGE

MATTHEW HYDE

The Silk Press
1999

On Stone by A F Tait.

Published by Bradshaw & Blacklock London & Manchester

VIEW from ALDERLEY EDGE.

(L.&N.W. RAILWAY.)

A splendid lithograph of the view from the Edge, made by A F Tait in about 1848. It has not changed so much today, although Manchester has got a lot closer. The railway features just as a very distant viaduct, slightly left of centre. The thatched cottage, centre, immediately below the Edge, also appears in the two postcard views that follow. Tait's 1845 lithographs of the Manchester and Leeds Railway sold well, but this series was never even published and in 1850 he emigrated to America, where he is celebrated as an artist of wildlife.

Courtesy National Railway Museum

ACKNOWLEDGEMENTS

This book is a gathering-together of all the information, stories and reminiscences that have been given to me by the people of Alderley Edge, and without them it could not have been written. My thanks are due first therefore to the people of Alderley Edge, especially those who have so kindly allowed me to see their houses, and those who have lent materials. I would also like to record my thanks and appreciation to all my colleagues on the Alderley Edge Landscape Project, who have made the work at Alderley Edge so enjoyable and mind-widening.

Special thanks are due to Gwen Comer, among many others, for her invaluable reminiscences of life on the Edge; to the Edge Association for permission to illustrate the visiting cards; to Anthony Gaddum for his fund of knowledge and splendid family archive; to my neighbour Basil Jeuda for his introduction to the world of publishing as well as on railway matters; to John Kempster for his local knowledge; to Rosemary Marsh, and to Pilkington's Tiles, for matters relating to Firwood and the Pilkington family; to George Twigg for his family's admirable propensity to photograph one another, as well as much practical information; to Jenny Youatt for all things pertinant to St Hilary's.

For their help and forbearing in the arduous business of preparing this book for publication I thank Colin Tucker and Christine Pemberton.

COPYRIGHT
AE 15

AT THE FOOT OF THE EDGE, ALDERLEY EDGE

LILYWHITE LTD
BRIGHOUSE

ALDERLEY EDGE.

These four postcard views of c1905 show the contrasting faces of Alderley Edge. These two, near the Hough on Mottram Road, show the untouched countryside as it must have been before the railway arrived. The thatched cottage appears in both views.

Courtesy Jackie Stone

Queen's Hotel and Station, Alderley Edge 47211

Meanwhile, at the station, carriages greet the incoming train from Manchester.
This view (was it taken from the steeple of St Philip's?) illustrates beautifully the social stratification of the new Alderley Edge.
Down below, on the flat, is the tightly packed village; up above on the verdant slopes of the Edge are the villas. The same shoulder of hill appears in the poscard opposite.

Courtesy Basil Jeuda

Alderley Edge.

Aerial view of St Philip's. The architect J S Crowther had great trouble with the patterned slate roof, and never repeated it. By the shadow of the spire is the original parsonage and at the far right is the school. Prominent to the north of the church is Brookdale, and behind that Oakleigh, with its gardener's cottage at the furthest top left. Across the main road on the right can be seen the cottages belonging to Brookdale that formed the nucleus of Tower Garage.

Private collection

Part One

HOW IT ALL BEGAN

Once there was a place called Alderley Edge, a weird and wonderful hill rising suddenly out of the gentle Cheshire plain, an outrigger of the Pennines but so distinctive in its geology and hence in its landforms and history as to take on a unique identity of its own. A place of mines and legends, and still, in spite of being so well known, capable of springing major surprises.

Two such surprises turned up in the 1990s. One was the chance finding of a hoard of Roman coins buried only a yard down in a mine shaft just by Engine Vein Mine, one of the most visited places on the Edge. The other was a rediscovery, of an old wooden shovel also found in a mine shaft, and featured in Dr JD Sainter's Scientific Rambles round Macclesfield of 1878 which has been recently republished by the Silk Press. This had hung on the schoolroom wall in Alderley Edge for years, then it was lost, then in limbo. When finally dated scientifically it turned out to be c1750 BC. The story is told by Alan Garner in his introduction to the reprint. The two finds, proving for the first time the great antiquity of the Alderley Edge mines, highlighted our ignorance about this most well-known spot and spawned the Alderley Edge Landscape Project that ran from 1996 to 1998. It was jointly run by the Manchester Museum and the National Trust. I was lucky enough to be part of that project and this book is a spin-off from it. Alderley Edge is still there of course, as weird and wonderful as ever. A large and increasing portion of it is owned and preserved for us all by the National Trust, and much enjoyed by everybody from dogwalkers to cavers, children on birthday outings to academics trying to make sense of it all.

Since 1842 there is a second Alderley Edge. A village with a tree-lined main street of unusually classy shops, backed by a tight grid of a few terraced streets on one side and more generously spaced middle-class housing on the other, and a remarkable villa-land, where large variegated houses stand in spacious and leafy gardens, connected by steep rocky roads. The villas are as romantic as the rest of the Edge, an essential part of its weirdness and wonderfulness. This is their story.

The story begins, as such stories will, with a man with a plan. Sometime in 1836, not long after the Liverpool and Manchester Railway had ushered in a new age of rapid travel for all, a surveyor came through this untouched bit of old England with a theodolite. He was prospecting for a new direct line between Manchester and Birmingham, in competition with the Grand Junction.

The new line had to skirt the Edge, a no-go area to railway engineers in search of the gentle gradient, cross the old south road, today's A34, and then swing left to Congleton and the Potteries. Another line was to branch from the main route at Alderley to join the Grand Junction at the same place as a projected line from Chester. That place had no name but it soon acquired one :- Crewe.

The two railway bills came before parliament and the new queen Victoria in 1837, but already ambitions for an independent through route had been compromised. By autumn 1839 they had been given up altogether; the branch to Crewe became the main line, and the route from Alderley to Congleton was abandoned. Not however before the footings of a great viaduct across the Dane valley at Congleton had been laid, with a ceremonial dinner and fireworks. The projected cost of this viaduct, weighed against the cost of another one at Holmes Chapel for the Crewe link, killed the scheme but there was also a deal of heavy persuasion from the Grand Junction.

The Manchester and Birmingham Railway had a brief but exciting existence as an independent company, before amalgamating with its old enemy, the Grand Junction, to form the LNWR. Railway history is a minefield and I would refer readers to the Railway Magazine for September and October 1960 for a full account by GO Rolt.

Getting a railway built was a complicated business. First a route had to be found to please both the promoters and the engineers. Then negotiations had to be made with all the landholders and interested parties along the way. Next the bill had to be brought before parliament, which required the services of a railway solicitor and a parliamentary agent. Capital had to be raised. Then came the business of building it, with armies of navvies to be found, fed, accommodated, and kept out of trouble. When the railway finally came to be opened it had to be promoted, stations opened and passenger and freight customers wooed.

It was on the 10th of May 1842 that the Manchester and Birmingham Railway opened to passengers. The day was an anticlimax because the Grand Junction, having talked the M&B out of its direct line from Alderley to the Potteries, had then double-crossed it, reneging on its agreement to allow M&B trains through from Crewe to Birmingham. So the first trains ran only from Manchester to Sandbach, via Stockport, Cheadle, Handforth, Wilmslow, Alderley, Chelford (where there were connecting coaches for Macclesfield and

Congleton), and Holmes Chapel.

The decision to open a station at Alderley was a surprising one because there was no significant settlement here. It was perhaps a survival of the original grand plan which would have featured a junction at this point.

So the 10th of May 1842 can be taken as the birthday of the new Alderley Edge.

It is time to introduce some of the protagonists in the story so far. There were two principal landlords:- Sir John, first Lord Stanley of Alderley, who owned most of the Edge itself and lands to the south and east of it; and Sir Thomas Joseph de Trafford whose Wilmslow estate reached the northern steeps of the Edge.

Lord Stanley is described as old, dirty and curmudgeonly but he was surrounded by intelligent, outspoken and articulate womenfolk, and it is thanks to some of their letters, collected by Nancy Mitford in The Ladies of Alderley and the Stanleys of Alderley that we can learn something of the negotiations between railway company and landholder.

Henrietta Maria Stanley to her mother-in-law, Lady Stanley, who was staying with her brother-in-law the bishop at Norwich; 8th September 1843;

"............as we were at luncheon yesterday we saw a man walk up whom his Lordship feared was a Parson. I feared a RailRoadian & so the case

STANLEY

proved, Mr Waddington Deputy Chairman B&M. He was shown into the drawing room, Ld S finished eating then went in desiring us to follow, we did so soon for we did not know what might happen.. now what do you think was the impudent man's proposal, that Lord Stanley should allow the managing clerk of the R.R. to give orders on one of our private days!"

The Railway company was pushing vigorously for business at its new station, and were requesting increased access to the beauties of the Edge. "Poor Edge! I feel one loves it more for the insecurity of the tenure". wrote Henrietta Maria in the same letter. She implies that it was to be for new residents only, in addition to the days when they allowed public access - "the cottontots forsooth prefer the days without a crowd."

The Stanleys were fond of playing with words. Not for nothing had they employed Edward Lear as a tutor. Cottontots is a new one. Describing the nouveaux riches coming in from Manchester it nicely marries the source of their money - cotton, hence business - with the supposed primitive and backward tribe the Hottentots. A wicked label, but useful.

Later in the same letter she refers to a Mr Westend; "Both this Waddington and Westend are just like Americans so free and easy." I think this is Stanley speak for Mr Easted, another

RailRoadian. The chairman of the company was Thomas Ashton who lived in a palatial villa filled with art, Ford Bank, at Didsbury. The chief engineer was George Watson Buck; perhaps the very man with the plan.

The railway company, in spite of their free and easy ways, got little joy from Lord Stanley. He refused to allow any land to be released for building, despite the urgings of his agent - (1 Sep 1844) *"Simpson told me he thought there would be a great advantage in laying out Chorley as Villas that it would quadruple the value of that part and improve the whole -"*, and resisted the further encroachment of visitors to the Edge. So the Stanleys and their lands play no part in the first phase of residential development of Alderley Edge.

It is worth noting, however, that they created considerable difficulties over its name. *"An interest almost national, owing to the notice taken by the London press, was in the year 1863, excited by the refusal of the post office authorities to recognise the existence of any such place as Alderley Edge, and the consequent non-delivery, until after much delay, of letters thus addressed. Meetings were held, and memorials were sent up in vain, until at last, a formidable guarantee fund was subscribed, for compelling the post office to send letters direct to the place, for which they knew only too well that such letters were intended. Perseverance prevailed, and Alderley Edge is now recognised by the post office authorities."*

This is from Morris & Co's Directory of 1874. It must have been a serious matter to appear in such a publication. The effect of this bizarre state of affairs is apparent even today to researchers who will search in vain for the census returns for Alderley Edge. You must look under Chorley.

Sir Edward was by now the second Lord Stanley of Alderley. He was the elder of twins - his brother Owen got the Penrhos estate and Holy Island in Anglesey, where his influence was to prove an interesting contrast to that of his brother. Lord Stanley himself was behind this vendetta. He was Postmaster-General. Fletcher Moss has the neatest comment on the affair, simply quoting drily in his sixth volume of *Pilgrimages to Old Homes* the good baron's epitaph:- *"(He) was always distinguished by clearness of judgement and by uncompromising public spirit."* Quite so. There was, however, some foresight in his action, for the name has caused confusion ever since, making it necessary to distinguish between Alderley Edge village and Alderley Edge *Edge*.

Negotiations between the agents of the railway and Sir Thomas de Trafford were much more fruitful.

The Traffords had held lands in Wilmslow parish, stretching down to Alderley Edge, since 1414 (see Earwaker *East Cheshire*). In 1402 a young boy, Richard Venables was drowned in the river Bollin at Ringway. He was heir to extensive lands in Wilmslow parish. As a result of his death the estates were divided between his two sisters, Alice and Douce. Douce married Sir Robert de Booth; The couple are commemorated by a charming brass kept under a carpet in Wilmslow parish church. Alice married Edmund Trafford. He was an alchemist.

The Traffords have never resided on their Wilmslow estate. They are an ancient Lancashire family whose principal seat was Trafford Park. This may surprise those who know Trafford Park as a great industrial estate, but so it was :- a large classical mansion with an older house behind, set in fine 700 acre park, walled about, and skirted by the limpid rivers Irwell and Mersey.

Thomas Joseph Trafford was born in 1803 not, however, at Trafford Park but at Croston near Chorley in Lancashire, the seat of a cadet branch of the family. The failure of the male line at Trafford meant that he inherited both estates, and Wilmslow to boot. In 1841 he was created baronet, and shortly afterwards obtained royal license to assume, or resume, the prefix 'de'.

The de Trafford papers are deposited in Lancashire Record Office at Preston. There are 610 boxes of them, unsorted and uncatalogued. Somewhere amongst them will be the whole story of the negotiations between Sir Thomas and the Railway. What has come to light so far is a box of diaries kept by his steward or agent, who does not name himself but is I think Mr Thomas Ayres. He was responsible for estate business at Trafford, Stretford, Barton, and at

DE TRAFFORD

Wilmslow and Alderley Edge but not at Croston.

What I like about diaries is their immediacy. Events are written on the very day they happen and we can see the very page and ink of that day:- *(11 June 1842) "In Manchester met the Barton church building committee fixed upon Pauling and Co to build the church their estimate 1695£. Went in the afternoon with the architect and Mr Cunningham to set out the statute area of land, Mr Welsh, the architect, took my tape with him."*

This refers to the building of St Catherine's Barton-on-Irwell. It is nice to think of the gentlemen measuring out in the fields the plot where the new church was to be, and one can still sense Mr Ayres' annoyance at the loss of his tape-measure. St Catherine's, though, has gone again. But diaries are very tantalising, because the diarist so often fails to pick out what proves to be important later. So for the 10th of May 1842, the very day that the Manchester and Birmingham Railway opened its station at Alderley we get just routine estate business in Barton. We do, however, get on May 5th 1842, *"Went to Wilmslow, met Mr Easted (Railway agent) and Mr Humphrey (de Trafford) about damage to tenants. Mr Easted informed me that ..... he wants to take the plan and go all along the line, and give enumeration (remuneration?) to every tenant that had sustained any damage by*

14

trespass .....” and on the 18th “ .....*a number of people came from Manchr by railway to the Alderley station.*”

Between them Sir Thomas and the agents of the railway agreed a strategy that was to determine the origin of Alderley Edge, its character as a posh satellite of Manchester, and the bounds by which it was contained. The Railway agreed to open a station and to build a hotel next to it. The de Traffords agreed to parcel up their lands into two and three acre plots and offer them for building, with stringent restrictions which were often summarised on later deeds as *‘for quiet enjoyment’*. The Railway Company capped it all by the splendid offer of a first class pass to the head of the household, provided the new house exceeded a certain value.

The idea of a free pass seems to have come from George Hudson, the famous railway king. He was a board member but tended to take a back seat at the company’s board meetings; however he influenced its policy considerably.

The package was irresistible. “ ...... *the greatest fog in Manchesr ...... but quite clear in Alderley.*” wrote Mr Ayres on 30th January 1843, and on New Year’s Eve, “..... *to Manchester, still frosty and very foggy.*” Who could resist, if they could afford it, escaping the filthy fogs of Manchester, that turned new buildings velvet black before they were even finished, for the wooded heights and clean air of Alderley Edge?

Development really started in 1845:-

(Jan 2 1845) “..... went to Manchr a Mr Gibbons and Mr Lewis at Mr Lee’s each bought a plot of land at Alderley, at 12-12- an acre.” But the land was not uninhabited:-

(Feb 10 1845) “Went to Alderley about tenants giving up land purchased for building by Messrs Gibbons, Farnworth, and Lewis, the land being wanted immediately the tenants expect some consideration for giving it up.”

We can be relieved to learn that they were not simply kicked out.

(10 March 1845) “ .... the tenants agreed to give up the land, ... to give them a bonus for doing so immediately, as per the agreem’t.”

An interesting entry follows.

(12 May 1845) “Went to Alderley, let clay to James Heath(?) of Heaton Norris for making brick and not to charge Sir Tho Trafford. Bart, more than 22/- a thousand for them.”

So it looks as though the de Traffords were considerably involved in the building process. There was much to be done.

(10 July 1845) “Went to Alderley with Mr Cuffly, Mr Farnworth, Mr Palin & Mr Gibbons, there I asked about the road there had been so much said about, between Mr F and Mr P - after a good deal of conversation upon it I advised they should each contribute to the forming and making the road, that is Mr Gibbons, Mr Farnworth, & Mr Palin, and to have a lodge next the Macclesfield land.”

The road in question is, I think, Woodbrook road. The reference to the lodge is interesting because it may refer to Ferns - now Franklyn - Lodge, which therefore would have served not one but a group of villas on the lines of Victoria Park, or Cressington Park in Liverpool. Mr Gibbons and Mr Farnworth appear repeatedly on Alderley Edge deeds.

Although Mr Ayres only allows us a tantalising glimpse every now and then amongst all his other estate business, it is fascinating to see a new community hesitantly starting and then rapidly growing before our eyes.

The first class pass, which would be worn on your watch-chain.
Courtesy National Railway Museum

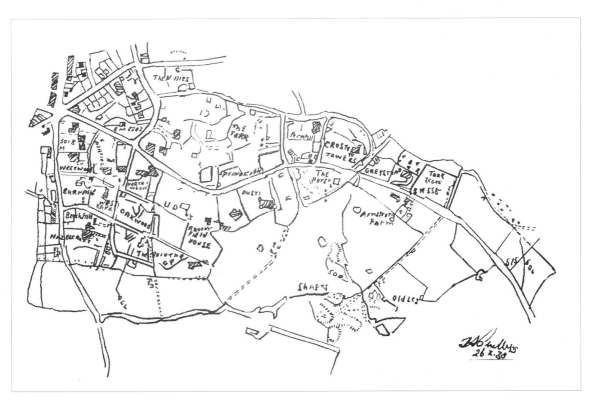

Abstract of title map, showing the villas at an early stage of development. The official version of this map is on pp62 and 63.

Sir Thomas Joseph, first baronet de Trafford, of Croston and Trafford Park (1778-1852). He set in motion the development of Alderley Edge.

Croston Hall in central Lancs, 1902. Sir Thomas's second son, John Randolphus, inherited the Croston estate in 1852 and soon set about replacing the modest hall where his father had been born with this pile, designed by Edward Pugin.

Courtesy Frances Ramsden

Sir Thomas's eldest son, Sir Humphrey de Trafford (1808-1886) inherited the principal seat at Trafford, plus Wilmslow and Alderley Edge.

Sir Humphrey and Lady Annette ready for the hunt at (believe it or not) Trafford Park. Just ten years after his death it became the world's first industrial estate.
  Courtesy Sir Dermot de Trafford

ELIZABETHIAN REVIVED.

RURAL ITALIAN.

Kell, Bro⁸ Lith

OSBORNE

MEDIÆVAL

COTTAGE

VILLA STYLE

What is a villa? It can be defined by what it is not. A farm is home and workplace to a farming family. Their livelihood is around them in the fields, their lives are entirely bound up in it. A cottage is the humbler dwelling of a family who live by hiring their labour; most probably to the farmer, but there may be some who weave and spin, and others who delve under the ground for copper and lead. The great house is the seat of the landed family. They own the lands on which the farmer and the cottager live. Their wealth and their prestige is that land and those people; without them they would be nothing. All are dependent one on another, from the humblest cottager to Lord Stanley himself. It is called feudalism.

Villas and villa-builders are different. They are in the country but not of the country, owing nothing to nobody. Their only ties are to the distant city, from whence the money comes. The villa is an escape from the noise and dirt of that city, but inescapably tied to it by the silver lines of the railway or the hot tarmac of the road.

The railway age engendered villas in great number, from commuter colonies around Manchester to retirement homes in Devon. However, the villa as a type has a surprisingly long ancestry. In Roman times villas abounded in the more attractive parts of the empire, once peaceful conditions had been securely established. Emperor Hadrian built a prodigious one at Tivoli, not too far from Rome. In the mid 16th century Palladio built them in the countryside of the Veneto for the rich merchants of Venice and Vicenza. In the 1720s Alexander Pope built one, and wrote about it, on the Thames above London. It was not far from Henrietta Howard's pretty Palladian villa, Marble Hill, and near to where Horace Walpole was soon to build his delectable gothick plaything, Strawberry Hill. These epithets could only really be applied to villas. There is often an element of fantasy about them, whether it is in their name, or their style, or the planting and ornamentation of the garden - or indeed all of these.

Farms and cottages don't have a style. They are vernacular buildings that spring naturally from the land and the culture that

20

produced them. The great house is not vernacular, it is Architecture, the work of an architect. Villas can be vernacular and they can be Architecture but usually they are not really either. They are, however, almost always dressed up in a style.

In 1864 Robert Kerr published a book called *The English Gentleman's House*. He was rather tiresome as an architectural pundit, and not very successful as a practitioner - *"my architect has no notion of aspect or prospect, and not much of respect"* said his greatest client, John Walter, bitterly -, but the lengthy section on style, illustrated as it is by his designs for the same house tricked out in ten different styles, would have been much consulted by builders and their clients in its day.

One of the Alderley Edge villas is styled as a Castle. Two or three are Cottages. A couple are Medieval and several, with less conviction, Elizabethan. There was even a Swiss one; but the majority are what he calls Rural Italian. The immediate prototype was Prince Albert's *Osborne*, begun in 1845, an engraving of which is the frontispiece of Robert Kerr's book. The fondness of the English, and Germans, for the type goes back to the paintings of Claude which were hugely collectible to 18th century gents. Sir George Beaumont carried his 'Pastoral landscape' about with him wherever he went, and they have been part of our cultural baggage ever since. The Italian villa, with its simple white walls and round-topped windows, its classical symmetry casually set off

by an asymmetrical tower, was inseparable from the idyllic countryside, the sunny skies, the contented peasants and animals that Claude depicted. Hence its popularity.

Edward Walters and John Edgar Gregan are the two architects particularly associated with the Italian style in Manchester, after its first essay by Barry at the Athenaeum in 1837. Walters' Free Trade Hall of 1853 is the star but the rows of warehouses lining Princess Street are its most typical expression - and the Italianate villas out at places like Alderley Edge. Firwood was designed by Gregan, and Underwood is another candidate. Walters may have designed Hazelcroft. Others could turn their hands to the style when required. Edward Starkey, architect, leased a plot on Heyes Lane in 1853 and built two villas on it. One has gone but the other, The Heyes, is so eminently typical that he may have had a hand in many more.

The alternative style, seen as somehow truer and definitely more English, was gothic. The great champion of gothic, and denouncer of all things classical - and Italianate - was AWN Pugin, that vociferous and eminently persuasive Catholic convert and firebrand. Many architects accepted his lead when it came to church work; Starkey for instance when he rebuilt the chancel of St Mary's in 1855. A few followed the philosophy of true gothic for everything. One such was JS Crowther, designer of St Philip's and the school, who built for himself a thoroughly gothic house to show it could be done - Redclyffe Grange. Crowther was a reserved and enigmatic man, nothing like Pugin, but the centre of a group of friends all with Alderley Edge connections :- Henry Bowman (the Whins), Thomas Worthington (Broomfield), Edward Salomans (Oakwood) and also AF Tait the lithographer.

When all is said and done it is unlikely that we will ever assign an architect's name to most of the villas. Once the desired style had been perfected it could be copied, with variations, by anybody.

The coming of the villas, each with its own little estate but not sustained by it, was more than just another chapter in the long history of the settlement of Alderley Edge. It was a new dimension, bringing it into the orbit of the city, and hence the world, for the first time. It is perhaps understandable that the indigenous Alderley Edgers of every degree should have felt some irritation at the invasion. The term 'cottontot', invented by the Stanleys, makes their opinion on the subject perfectly clear. The de Traffords, as absentee landlords, were in a more equivocal position. The centre of their interests was elsewhere. They were also perhaps unusually willing to change with the times.

Looking far ahead, however, we should note that the country has its own strength and its own way of working a slow change upon those who come to live in it. As the delights and distractions of the country places where the bosses now lived took hold, so the industries of Manchester lost their cutting edge. The next generation of cottontot children, born in Alderley or Bowdon or Lymm, sent away to school, and then to university, lost interest in the gritty city that had nurtured their parents and grandparents, and lost empathy with its workforce. As the city expanded and fragmented so it slowly lost its power; only very recently is the process turning around.

Conversely, the city has had all too obvious an effect on Alderley, as it has almost everywhere in Cheshire and indeed in much of England. To begin with the area of the villas was neatly circumscribed but now any farm or cottage that comes up for sale is liable to gentrification. Today even fifty or sixty acres of good Cheshire land does not generate enough income to support a farm family. So they are being turned into villas.

Alderman John Hopkinson of Manchester, whose children all emigrated to the new villa suburbs (see Ferns).

The Heyes is typical of the smaller Italianate villas, although it stands a little isolated on Heyes Lane. Note the alternating iron and wooden balusters to the fine staircase. The wine cellar is always under the front hall.

The Heyes -
Far left: Staircase, and
Left: The cellar

A corner of the dining room of Firwood, with an evening view of the trees on the Edge and the plain far below.

Courtesy Phyllis Redding

Gardeners pose outside Beechfield, c1913. We may suppose that the headgardeners wear bowlers, the undergardeners flat hats. Standing second from the left, with prominent watch-chain, is John Twigg; kneeling in front of him, in a light suit, is Fred Dutton, and on the back row, second from the right, is Arthur Hobson.

Courtesy George Twigg

A rare survival into 1999, a complete maids' bathroom. It is at the Hollies. It may look uninviting, but a room of your own and use of a proper bathroom would have been a major inducement to go into service.

LIFE IN THE VILLAS

The day started early for the indoor servants; there were fires to be lit and breakfasts to prepare. Typically there were four or five indoor servants, all unmarried women. The housemaid would set the table for their own breakfast in the kitchen or, occasionally, a servants' hall, at the back of the house. They would sit in strict order of seniority to eat. A very few of the houses had a butler; he would be waited on at table.

The gardeners started early too, checking temperatures and ventilation in the various greenhouses and stoking the furnaces. They would have breakfasted at home, but would have some sort of a bothy for a brew later.

The family would assemble for breakfast which would be quite a substantial meal. Most of the big houses had a breakfast room which would be relatively cosy with a window to catch the morning sun. A few of the houses held family prayers first - Oakhurst for instance. This would be a ceremonial affair with the servants filing in and out in reverse order of seniority.

The gentlemen left for their daily journey up to Manchester. There were three trains, the "striving, thriving and thriven" after the old rhyme "he that would thrive must rise at five.,etc". They tended to use not just the same train but the same carriage every day, which soon became a sort of club. So the half-hour journey was by no means wasted time, either socially or in business terms (see The Meadows).

During term time most of the elder children would be away at boarding school, although some would travel each day to Manchester Grammar School. Parents were determined that their offspring should receive the education that they and their parents had perhaps lacked. They would return home for the hols with posh accents and posh friends. The younger children might be at school in the village, perhaps at Miss Barton's in Stamford Road.

Breakfast over and the breadwinners gone, relative quiet falls. There was always plenty of work to be done in the house, each of the servants having their allotted tasks and responsibilities. Travellers would call, come to take orders from the local shops, which would be brought up later by delivery boys from the village. There would be plenty of tradesmen about - always a sign of a well-to-do neighbourhood:- carpenters and masons busy with alterations and extensions, decorators come to measure up for curtains and papers.

The lady of the house having given her orders might venture forth into the garden, where she would always be obliged to consult the head gardener before so much as picking a few flowers; or, suitably hatted and gloved, go down to the village. She would always go to the front of the queue in the shops, and be charged accordingly, but then everything went on account so it is hard to know who was conning who.

Let us pause a moment and listen to the drowsy daytime sounds of the Edge :- the twitter of a few birds and rustle of leaves; the very characteristic and penetrating pok...pok of tennis - there is always someone playing - down at the club; the clear sound of men at work on a roof somewhere - their voices, the slither and clatter of slates, the clink of tools; an occasional rumble of wheels on one of the cobbled hills, the drone of a mower.

Meanwhile the men had dispersed to their various mills and offices in the vast workshop that was Manchester. Alderley Edge needs to be seen in the context of the teeming city, so busy, so dirty, so noisy but so rewarding. Competition was fierce, technology advancing at a breakneck pace, labour relations often difficult, but there were fortunes to be made.

They might meet up again for lunch at the Union Club, next to the City Art Gallery on Mosley Street, or the Clarendon nearby. These had the most social cachet; the Reform Club on King Street slightly less so despite its splendid building.

Back at home in the gardens there were lawns to cut, vegetables and fruit to tend, and endless jobs to do in the potting sheds and glasshouses. The gardeners, unlike the indoor servants, were usually locals as can be seen by their indigenous names. Sometimes they lived in a lodge or gardener's cottage but more commonly they had their own homes down in the village. After the lunch break many of them would gather outside the Trafford Arms and wait for Massey's one o'clock hooter before dispersing again to the various gardens. The situation is not so very different today.

A major obligation, which occupied the ladies for two or three afternoons a week was that of calling on ones neighbours. This was not a simple matter. Cards had to be left and returned in the prescribed order before one could 'know' one's neighbours. Both Margaret Pilkington and Katharine Chorley in their reminiscences (see Firwood and Ferns) are notably flustered by it all, even years afterwards.

There might be an occasion to use the carriage, or later on the car. Most of the villas sported a small stable block, with accommodation for a carriage of some description, a couple of loose boxes, and a tiny dwelling marked today by not much more than a ladder stair and a fireplace. However not many coachmen are listed and it is likely that, like the gardeners, they lived out. Indeed it seems that often the horses were hired too - see Brookdale.

The weary gentlemen returned home from the city by the 5.07pm or the 5.30pm train, walked up the darkening hill to the welcome lights of home. There might be time for a turn around the garden, even a game of croquet in the summer, before dinner.

Dinner was formal. One was required to dress even if no company was expected, gathering first in the drawing room. There were frequent dinner parties, quite grand affairs with six or seven courses. The progress of such a party was governed by rigid custom, the conversation controlled by the hosts until the sexes separated after the meal, the ladies returning to the drawing room, the gentlemen lingering at table and then perhaps going through for a game of billiards. No-one could describe these Alderley Edge dinner parties better than Katharine Chorley in her chapter on Ferns in 'Manchester Made Them'.

Let us listen with the head of the household for a minute, before he locks the big door after bidding the guests goodnight, to the night sounds. The wind breathes in the trees through which a big moon is rising, an owl hoots and creatures rustle in the undergrowth. Mist is rising from the lawns. Prosaic Manchester seems a long way off and the mysterious Edge alarmingly real and close.

On Sundays the routine was different. The family would walk out together to church, leaving the servants to prepare Sunday lunch. Many walked down to St Philip's or to the churchy Wesleyan chapel, others cut across and through the fields to St Mary's. The few Unitarian families who kept up their separateness, such as the Worthingtons at Broomfield, walked or rode to Dean Row chapel, and the Quakers such as the Satterthwaites at Fairfield went to the meeting house in Wilmslow.

On Sunday afternoon the servants, in rotation, would have a few hours of free time. Few could visit their families, for they were recruited from far and wide. The Institute in the village was built in 1878 to provide harmless - and alcohol-free - entertainment for the servants, but many preferred to walk over to Wilmslow or Macclesfield. Many attended the evening service at St Philip's, when all the seats were free - unlike the morning service; others walked out as far as Birtles church to enjoy the air and freedom. The gardeners and coachmen were free to spend the day with their families and relations, to attend chapel at the Hough, do the odd 'foreigner' to earn a bit of cash or as a favour, have a drink at the Trafford Arms, or play in the St Philip's brass band. Someone would have to be back at night however, to check the glasshouses, stoke the furnaces and close the vents.

The villas that were built in the railway age, on de Trafford land, are listed in two gazetteers; the longer one of the villas on the hill, and a much shorter one of a contemporary but physically separated group near the station.

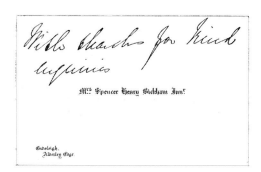

Butler's pantry at Westwood, complete with cupboards and drawers, a sink, and a safe - but not necessarily a butler. Most houses had an all-female indoor staff.

Mr L Hacker, gardener, of Moss Lane. He worked for the Handasyde-Dick family. This photograph was taken in the 1920s at one of the houses in the Horseshoe, but they later moved to Ashfield. *Courtesy George Twigg*

St Hilary's girls on the lawns of Westwood. The photo is from a school brochure of 1965.
Courtesy Jenny Youatt

Sunday School boys are welcomed at Ferns by Mr Fred Rowcliffe c1896. Daniel Twigg is sitting at the right-hand end.
Courtesy George Twigg

This is where the money came from. A rare set of photographs of JF & H Roberts' mill at Oxenhope c1920 (see Oakhurst p128/9).
Courtesy Anthony Gaddum

Weaving shed

Despatch Department

Some of the workers

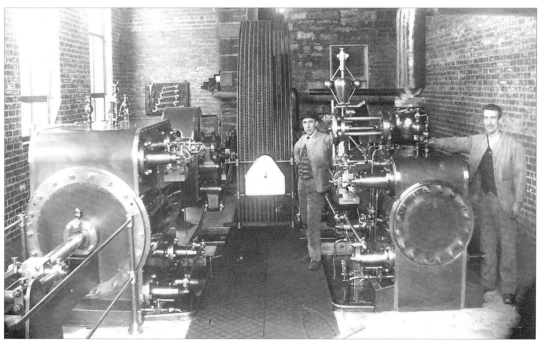

The Engine House

St Phillips Brass Band
Courtesy George Twigg

Mosley Street Manchester. Beyond the City Art Gallery is the Union Club, favoured lunching-place of the cottontots. The photograph is not dated but there are plenty of clues in costume and transport. The Union Club amalgamated with the Clarendon c1962 and was closed and demolished not long after.
Courtesy Chris Makepeace

Sunday and holiday outings to the Edge were always immensely popular, and were encouraged by the Stanleys even while they were resisting allowing the cottontots further access.

Courtesy Basil Jeuda

FOR

SUNDAY SCHOOL & PLEASURE PARTIES

WITHIN EASY ACCESS FROM MANCHESTER.

Engraved by W.Banks, Edin.

The Knoll Ambleside,
The residence of

H. Martineau.

L.Aspland Del.t   W.Banks Sc. Edin.

AN INTERLUDE:
ALDERLEY EDGE AND WINDERMERE

Alderley Edge attracted the more adventurous of Manchester souls. Five years after the railway reached and opened up Alderley Edge, history repeated itself at Windermere - but with the considerable difference of a hundred mile journey compared with fourteen. Windermere attracted just the same kind of people, but more so. The parallel is very striking.

In 1847 a terminus opened at a place called Birthwaite, not far from the great lake of Windermere. The Railway Company chose to name their station Windermere, and that became the name of the resultant village and surrounding villa-land. Not without considerable controversy at the time, and the cause of some confusion ever since.

A rail traveller familiar with Alderley Edge will experience a strange feeling of deja vu on arrival at Windermere. There outside the station is the big hotel; here is the village street, dominated by banks not pubs, with short streets of terraced houses behind it. Soon one is out in a leafy, evergreeny semi-country dotted with villas, each one set just so to catch the view and the sun. But no lake. The unwary traveller is understandably vexed to find out that Windermere itself is a good two miles away.

The banks, the church, and the villas will look familiar too, although they have a different colour and texture because of the local stone, and they have much more interesting names. The development of Windermere took a very similar course to that of Alderley Edge, although it was less parochial, having links with Liverpool and Leeds as much as Manchester; and of course the scenery is not just nice but world-beating. But it is more than parallel evolution because a number of the same people appear in both places. JS Crowther was the first of several architects to establish links. Having established a gothic presence at Alderley Edge he did the same at Windermere but on a bigger scale, with major works on several churches and a string of gothic villas. JR Lingard owned one at both places, see St Mary's Cliffe. Several families moved on from Alderley Edge to Windermere, or had houses in both places - the Gaddums (St Mary's Cliffe) who built Brockhole, the Groves (The Larches) who bought Holehird, the Milnes (Penn) who commissioned Dawstone. A few made the reverse journey, notably the Satterthwaites of Fairfield, and George Tunstall Redmayne, architect, of Brookside. Alfred Waterhouse gained his first architectural commission in 1855 through the Redmaynes of Brathey on Windermere. Young George Redmayne was to became one of Waterhouse's few pupils, then his Manchester partner and the husband of his sister Catherine.

Fallbarrow.

The Lake District exerts a powerful influence on those who make their homes there. It was perfectly possible to make the daily journey to Manchester but we can understand the urge to stay. Hence we might connect a further downturn in Manchester's industrial might with this more distant exodus.

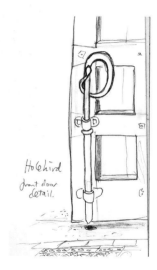

Holehird front door detail.

The villas of Windermere are one of the Lake District's unsuspected treats. Every one is beautifully placed, there is plentiful variety of style and there have been lots of entertaining owners; the air is good and one always has the bonus of distant fells and sparkling water. They have fared better than the villas of Alderley Edge because there are more modern uses open to them - hotel, outdoor centre, youth hostel - although many are still homes.

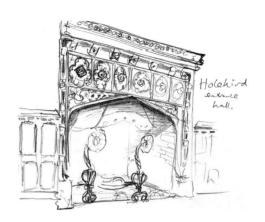

Holehird entrance hall.

Wynlass Beck

Cedar Manor, now a small Hotel, is said to have been the Windermere base of JS Crowther of Alderley Edge. Most of the houses illustrated here are his work, exhibiting all the same details as his Alderley houses. (see Redclyffe Grange).

Holehird has multiple connections with Alderley Edge. In the 1850s joint residence, with St Mary's Cliffe, of Mr Lingard; designed, as St Mary's Cliffe almost certainly was, by Mr Crowther; and the residence in the 1890s of Mr Groves, formerly of the Larches.
In 1889 Beatrix Potter's family took Holehird for the summer.

Far left: detail of a portrait of Henry, 3rd Lord Stanley.
Courtesy Lord Stanley

Left: This strange stone marks the spot of his burial in 1903 according to Muslim rites.

Far left: Pair of cottages built during Henry Stanley's baronetcy.

Left: Newspaper photograph of 12 October 1928, showing Arthur, 5th Lord Stanley, with his son Edward.

THE VILLAS OF ALDERLEY EDGE -
THE SECOND GENERATION

By 1900 Alderley Edge had developed into a compact village and a well-defined villa-land. Its boundaries were determined by the boundaries of the de Trafford estate. Beyond those boundaries the Stanley estate stayed much as it always had been. It had passed on the death of the first Lord Stanley in 1850 to the second baron, the twin, and in 1869 to his eldest son Henry. All three were opposed to change, despite the urgings of Mr Simpson their estate agent that they should lay out the Chorley Hall portion for villa development. It is worth noting that the copper mines on the Edge were active all through this period.

Henry was an interesting character. All nine of his family were interesting actually - they are beautifully portrayed on a brass in St Mary's church - but he is the most enigmatic. He looks in his portrait a little like King Ludwig of Bavaria - a big shy man in a big overcoat, full of suppressed fire. Henry was deaf. It cut him off from his fellows all his life. At an early age he conceived a great fascination for all things oriental - one can just imagine him, lonely and persecuted by his cruelly witty siblings, seeking refuge in the books in the family library. This was to lead him to learn Arabic, spend a lot of his life wandering in the east, and to become a muslim. This was an extraordinary thing to do in the 19th century, though not so very extraordinary in the context of his own family.

He married a very unsuitable lady, Fabia. So very unsuitable was she that not only did it transpire that she was a Roman Catholic, but that she had a husband already. Poor Henry went through at least three weddings with her, one at Macclesfield St Alban's, but none of them were any good. It is hardly surprising that the family have disowned her completely, and Henry as far as possible. So it is very difficult to ascertain what works if any were set in train on the estate during the thirty years that Henry and Fabia were Lord and Lady Stanley. This at a time when estates all over England were being improved and developed, none more so than that of their immediate neighbours the de Traffords.

The only notable estate developments attributable to them are a pair of cottages on Welsh Row and a single one on Slade Lane.

These are typically picturesque, using a vernacular vocabulary that is derived from books, not from the actual local vernacular, and very pretty they are too. The most surprising thing is that, despite their religious divergences, both Henry and Fabia did invest in the church in the approved manner. The organ in St Mary's church bears a small brass plate recording that it was given by Fabia, Lady Stanley in 1875. Who gave the oak pews, each with its own carved end-panel? Whose was the big Italian majolica image of the virgin and child (now in the Mausoleum) that is so unlikely an object in an English church at the time? Henry, despite his muslim faith, is known to have carried out church improvements in the way squires were supposed to do. But they are on his uncle's estate in Anglesey, at Lanbadrig on the north coast, and St Cybi Holyhead, and probably also at Valley. His work is distinctive because it does look Arabic. Turquoise tiles line the chancel at Llanbadrig, a most unlikely addition to this ancient church, and the sun makes strange patterns through the abstract glass. Above his uncle's marble tomb at St Cybi a strange note is provided by Henry's stained glass window of densely packed foliage and fruit only - no representation of the human figure.

Henry, 3rd baron Stanley of Alderley, died in 1903. He is buried not, of course, in a christian graveyard, but in a copse opposite the park. His lonely tombstone, which is carved with flowers in a completely unconventional way, is a moving sight amongst the rhododendrons and bracken, with the diggings of an active badger sett all around and a gloomy pool in juxtaposition. He was succeeded by his fourth brother Lyulph. Now, and only now, did the residential development of Alderley Edge touch the Stanley estate.

Lyulph was a man of socialist leanings, a follower of William Morris with an interest in the ennobling principle of the Arts and Crafts and hand labour. It is not surprising that the second wave of villa development he set in train is different in kind from the first.

First came a couple of houses at the top of Macclesfield Road, Edgecroft and Greylands. These are not significantly different from the previous generation, and Edgecroft's neat stable places it still in the age of horses and carriages. Soon however came Penn, and then Abbott Brow, definitely 20th century, built by Massey's with the best craft methods, and designed by two of the sons of old Thomas Worthington of Broomfield. See the gazetteer for details of these houses.

In about 1909 plots were laid out all along the Congleton Road and White Barn Road for villa development, although it took a few years for all the plots to be built on. In landscape terms the development is disappointing; the age of the motor car was dawning and the road was the important thing. So this is ribbon development and little pleasure is to be had from walking around it. But the houses are good. I think we owe this to Lord Stanley himself. He saw to it that architects were employed and he approved their designs himself. Among them were members of two well-known local dynasties :- Percy and Hubert Worthington the eldest and youngest sons of Thomas Worthington of Broomfield, and the three generations of the Fairhursts. This phase saw the rise to local dominance of Isaac Massey & Sons as the excellent builders they became.

These new houses are cottage-style, low-ceilinged, homely. The doors are planked, with iron latches, the windows latticed. The roofs sweep down comfortably and the walls are finished in a plain white roughcast. They are also spacious and gracious, and have all the convenience brought by electricity, modern plumbing and central heating. Servant accommodation is still provided but these houses are designed to be easy to run. It is a case of having your cake and eating it.

Massey's yard spread along the railway, behind the Streets. *Author's collection*

Apprentices made a test piece such as this miniature sash window made by Daniel Twigg.

44

Penn on a 'gardens open' day in 1994. It was very popular.

Wedding of Percy Worthington and Lucy Juliet Wolff, 1895. Thomas Worthington (see Broomfield) sits centre right with his legs crossed with his youngest son Hubert by his side.

Courtesy Anthony Pass

34 Congleton Road, alias Greythwaite, front elevation.
It was designed by Harry Fairhurst in 1909.
Courtesy Nick & Julie Clayton

The proportions of the front seem to work better on a drawing than in three dimensions.
The garden side and plan are on p146.

The war memorial outside St Philip's. The many names of the fallen are set all around on bronze plates.

This brief inscription is let into the pavement at the foot of the memorial.

EMILY F. A. HUTTON. O.B.E.
FOR FOUR YEARS COMMANDANT
OF THE BROOKDALE AUXILIARY
MILITARY HOSPITAL
ALDERLEY EDGE
DIED 9TH FEBRUARY 1919

During both world wars house-building came to a standstill. In the Second World War Mr Beresford, designer of charming Arts-and-Crafts houses such as Hill Cottage, turned his hands to pre-fabs. This one, the Cornish Unit, was remarkably successful, and a number are still going strong long after their projected time span.

Courtesy Roger and Elaine Williams

THE VILLAS IN WARTIME

Edwardian England was a golden age in many ways, nowhere more so than in the big houses of Alderley Edge. Never again would life be so gracious, gardens so immaculate, the meritocracy so confident. The two great world wars of the 20th century affected everybody and changed things for ever.

Soon after 1914 the men volunteered for war. The cottontot families were, I suppose, more go-ahead than most; their sons volunteered with alacrity, were seen as officer material. Officers led from the front in the carnage that was trench warfare. So they got killed first. Read the names on the war memorial in front of St Philip's.

Desperately wounded men were brought back from the front. A hospital was set up here, in Alderley Edge, in Brookdale opposite the Tower Garage. Emily Hutton of Woodlands acted as commandant for the whole duration of the war, and is remembered by an inscription at the foot of the war memorial. Many of the wives and daughters volunteered to help with the nursing, among them the young Margaret Pilkington of Firwood. The tenants' hall at Alderley Park was used as a hospital too.

On a more material note, Massey's the builders were just getting into their stride with the second wave of villa building. Suddenly they were left with half-completed houses on their hands, building plots ready, a labour force that was disappearing day by day and no buyers. Massey's survived, but it was only by buying-in or renting finished houses, and, it seems, through the goodwill of Lord Stanley who commissioned the restoration of several of the ancient buildings of the estate - painstaking work that could be done by the older men who were left.

The 20s were a time of recession; strikes delayed building and rebuilding operations, even here among Massey's workforce. An unknown young man, we can allow ourselves to imagine a veteran of the Royal Flying Corps, flew a series of photographic sorties over northern England. His two shots of Alderley Edge, taken with a full plate camera in 1927, show the villas apparently untouched, each looking like a mini stately home in its two-acre park. There were still hardly any cars - only one is visible in the entire village centre, parked opposite the methodist church. Things were beginning to change though. The glasshouses, such a feature of the villas in their prime, were rapidly disappearing. During the war they had fallen cold, the precious orchids had died, and now the skilled labour was no more. Only the camellias proved that they had never needed mollycoddling; they flourish still in the ruins of the old greenhouses, as at Hazelcroft for instance.

Indoors too 'the servant problem' became increasingly acute. Most households had employed four or five servants, mostly unmarried young women. During the war many women took on what had previously been men's jobs. Never again would they be satisfied with a servant's lot.

The second world war came right home. Everywhere was a potential target. Children were evacuated immediately from the cities to safer country areas. The log book for Alderley Edge Infant School reports *(1 Sep 1939) "School closed at noon. National emergency. School closed for the week ending September 8th owing to the outbreak of war with Germany and the evacuation of children from Levenshulme."* When the school re-opened it was on a shift system, using a variety of other buildings around the village. Norwood, staffed by the Red Cross, was used as a canteen and clinic, and served at times for some of their schooling.

Manchester's blitz finally came two days before Christmas 1940. A stray stick of bombs destroyed Acton Farm, on Bradford Lane. Harold and Mary Worth, and an uncle who was calling for milk, were killed - they are buried in Birtles churchyard - but the children survived under the kitchen table. The bombing was at its most intense in early 1941, when the glow of the fires in Manchester and Liverpool could be clearly seen from the towers and rooftops of the villas. On February 5th the Council School reports *"Miss Benison absent owing to house being demolished by direct hit from bomb which caused the death of her mother and sister."* An incendiary bomb fell on the School too, during the Christmas holiday 1941, but the damage doesn't sound too bad :- *"Windows (five panes broken), table burnt, chair leg broken, wooden block floor burnt near fireplace, and sewing basket including contents destroyed."* During 1941 more evacuees had arrived from Wallasey, and in April 1942 came thirty-eight children, and their teachers, from the Channel Islands which were occupied by the Germans. Yet more were sent up from London during 1943.

Preparations for D-Day mobilised the whole country. It was England's greatest hour of need, but no knights in shining armour on white horses issued forth from the Iron Gates of the Edge, as some, mindful of the legend, might have hoped. It is strange the power of these old stories. Our own family, reared on *'The Weirdstone of Brisingamen'*, when driving across the Edge late at night in our old Landrover often used to imagine the wizard stopping us for a slightly more up-to-date steed. We were only 95% joking.

Instead came General George Patton and the 150,000 soldiers of the American 3rd army. General Patton set up his command a few miles away at Peover Hall, which is much smaller now than it was then because a large Georgian section was demolished in 1964. At Alderley Edge Americans were billeted at Ashfield, The Hurst, St Mary's Cliffe and others of the big houses, bringing their glamour and boldness, their candy, cigarettes, nylons and jeeps, and some innovations that are now familiar such as the Donut Dugout in Knutsford Town Hall.
Patton was also supposedly in command of an army gathering in the southeast, opposite the Pas de Calais; it was a phantom army of cardboard tanks, wooden guns and fake radio messages - all designed to obfuscate the enemy about the exact time and place of the invasion.

British soldiers of the Royal artillery were stationed at Cherrytree and several others down the hill - see Cherrytree in the gazetter. Units of the King's Liverpool Regiment were billeted in houses in Woodbrook Road.

For a while village life, especially for the girls, was very exciting. But soon after June 6th 1944 they all disappeared.

All over England iron railings disappeared 'to help the war effort'. Old photographs reveal just how much that changed the look of our towns. Here in Alderley Edge railings were never a dominant feature, but lots of the villas had cast iron balusters. Today these always alternate with plain wooden ones - was this a

wartime sacrifice? Many of the villas suffered during their wartime occupation, and the post-war years were a low time in their fortunes, but the losses here were nothing like so grievous as among the great country houses of England.

Sir Dermot de Trafford stands by a fine carving of the de Trafford arms, complete with a little thrasher on top and the words NOW THUS; August 1999.

The last days of Oakleigh, 20th August 1999.

IN WHICH THE STORY IS BROUGHT UP TO DATE

We have seen how the de Traffords leased off their lands in Alderley Edge for building from 1842. Initially the yield from ground rents was excellent but the rents were fixed and are hardly worth collecting today. Many of the leases have been bought out, others have lapsed by default, so the family's involvement in the area today is minimal.

Trafford Park itself had been encroached upon by the Bridgewater canal and the famous Barton aqueduct in 1761 but in 1896 came a much greater threat in the shape of the Manchester Ship Canal. Already the amenities of the Park were seriously blighted by what we would now recognise as acid rain. Sensing dissolution and acting with the same pragmatism that they had shown with the coming of the railway at Alderley Edge the family decided to pull out. Sir Humphrey (the second) and his widowed mother Lady Annette made a deal with Mr Ernest Hooley to sell the entire park for industrial development for £360,000 over the heads of the corporation. So after 900 years occupation they realised the enhanced value of their unproductive home, true to the family motto NOW THUS.

Their other Lancashire seat at Croston, a great gothic pile by Edward Pugin, was left to the Catholic archdiocese of Liverpool by the last squire of that line, Geoffrey de Trafford. His sister Ermyntrude lived on at the hall, crippled with arthritis and restricted to a single room, until 1964 when she died. Whereupon the archdiocese demolished the mansion and sold the estate. So that was the end, to all intents and purposes, of one of Lancashire's oldest landed families. What remains are the proud Catholic churches, all designed by Edward Pugin, at Barton, at Stretford, and at Croston, each one bearing the initials, crest, and portrait of the de Trafford donors.

Sir Dermot de Trafford, 6th and present baronet, lives in a charming village in Hampshire. His uncle Humphrey, the third one of that name and 4th baronet, had four children; but they were all girls, so by the inexorable laws of primogeniture the title went to his brother Sir Rudolph and then his nephew. Hanging on the stairs in the house is an astonishing picture of Sir Humphrey, 2nd Bt, and two of his brothers out hunting with the Lady Annette, with fine horses and a clutch of hounds, a herd of deer visible in front of the distant hall. Rolling parkland, old trees, rooks in the sky. Astonishing because the place is Trafford Park. I have stood on the same spot and tried to visualise it, but it is frankly unbelievable, so complete is the transformation. (see p17)

The Stanleys of Alderley resisted the blandishments of the railway company and the opportunities of residential development until it was too late to make a lot of money from it. Agricultural depression had by then shrunk their income, war and depression set back the economy, and now they were hit by two successive sets of death duties in 1925 and 1931.

Edward 6th Lord Stanley, not the finest flower of the English aristocracy, was saddled with a huge rambling mansion in Alderley Park; this particular problem was solved by a fire in 1931 followed by demolition of most of it. He may have hoped to redeem his finances by marrying Victoria, sister of the Earl of Shrewsbury but the marriage was not a success and they divorced in 1936.

In 1938 the entire Stanley holdings at Alderley were put up for sale. Every cottage and farm was pasted with a lot number. On the pattern of the existing developments on Congleton Road hundreds of building lots had been identified, in ribbons along every available access road. After five centuries of conservative Stanley ownership it was a major shock.

The sale itself, held over three days in October at the Stanley Hall Macclesfield, was an extraordinary fiasco. The papers were full of the Munich crisis and many were fearful for the future. The tenants turned up en masse, but not to bid. Instead they sat in rows in frozen silence. The hoped-for developers failed to materialise. Proceedings never got off the ground, and very little sold. A number of private treaties were made after the sale whereby tenants bought out their own farms without the threatened residential encroachment. Ribbon development was set in train along Bradford lane and Sandy lane but nothing like what was intended, for which we can be thankful.

Lyulph, 7th Lord Stanley, was as bad as his brother. He sold the Penrhos estate in 1948. The site of the mansion is occupied by Rio Tinto Zinc.

Thomas, 8th and present Lord Stanley of Alderley lives and farms in Anglesey. He is the third son of the third son, never thinking that he would inherit the title. The position of his farm in the rather bleak Anglesey landscape, dotted with wind generators, is intensely interesting because it lies right in the shadow of a mountain of copper - Parys Mountain. It was the chance discovery in 1768 of this most rich source that led Charles Roe to abandon his mining ventures at Alderley Edge. It seems fitting.

The railway company is a company once

again after fifty years of nationalisation. First NorthWestern operate the stopping trains between Manchester and Crewe. Passenger and freight trains of other companies roar through without stopping. There are a few more trains serving Alderley Edge than in 1843 and they are timetabled to make the journey to Manchester a little faster but the net gain is less than one might have hoped given the advance in technology. Alderley Edge station no longer plays a vital part in the economy of the place, especially since the building of a dual carriageway road link all the way from the Wilmslow border to Levenshulme, but the fortunes of public transport everywhere are showing signs of revival.

What of the villas? Eighty-odd are listed here. Out of that number some seventeen have gone. This includes one or two that are keenly to be regretted, such as St Mary's Cliffe and Swiss Cottage, and one, Oakleigh, that has been destroyed while this book was in preparation. So there is no cause for complacency - the two houses soon to be vacated by St Hilary's are clearly at risk - but Alderley Edge does seem to have kept its character and ambience better than most such places. It was after all notoriously publicised as the champagne capital of England only a year or two ago. Many of the remaining villas are subdivided, but expensive maintenance contracts ensure that the grounds don't get tatty. There are lots of infill houses but they have kept to the original de Trafford parcels and are mostly not too painful; some

indeed are quite interesting in their own right. A proportion of the villas are still in single family occupation, and long may this continue. Alderley Edge has managed somehow to keep its cachet in a world that is radically different from that of 1842. It must say something about the intrinsic attraction of the place itself, the old immemorial Edge, that place of gnarled rocks and anthropomorphic trees, of stunning views and labyrinthine mines, and an otherworldly quality that can still surprise us sometimes out of our everyday existence.

next to
Bishop's
Lodge
21 Sep 99
MH

disused Voysey gate
Woodbrook
MH

The Earl of Shrewsbury escorting his sister to her London wedding to Lord Stanley of Alderley.

PEER'S CATHEDRAL WEDDING

A collection of press cuttings documenting the wedding on 8 March 1932 of Edward 6th Lord Stanley and Lady Audrey Chetwynd-Talbot, sister of the Earl of Shrewsbury. The pictures are pretty but it was not a happy marriage; they divorced in 1936. Nor were Lord Stanley's financial affairs much better; he had demolished most of Alderley Park in 1933, and in 1938 he was forced to put the entire estate up for sale.

October 1928; The Hon. Edward Stanley with the oldest tenants, including Mrs J Massey.

This picture was sub-headed FAMILY TRADITIONS IN SAFE KEEPING.
The oldest tenants are presented to the new Lady Stanley.

The top two pictures show the newlyweds.
The wedding was at Southwark Cathedral.
Below we see the young couple after
attending morning service at Alderley the
following week, and their only child Edwina
who was born in 1933.

LORD STANLEY HOLDS THE BABY

Lord Stanley and
Alderley Park

Alderley Park -
South west front

ALDERLEY EDGE — CHESHIRE

Illustrated Particulars with Plans and Conditions of Sale

of the

ALDERLEY PARK ESTATES

MANCHESTER 15 miles; ALDERLEY EDGE 1 mile; MACCLESFIELD 5 miles;

extending to an area of about

4,624 Acres

and comprising

"ALDERLEY PARK"

with nearly 400 Acres, Gardens and Parklands

77 FARMS, all in a good state of cultivation

166 HOUSES and COTTAGES   "THE OLD HALL"

"HEAWOOD HALL"   "BOLLINGTON GRANGE"

"CHORLEY HALL"   "SOSSMOSS HALL"

Freehold Ground Rents   Woodlands and Plantations

Many Valuable BUILDING SITES including the famous
ALDERLEY EDGE and WIZARD WOODS
with glorious views

The whole producing an actual income of

£9,699 Per Annum

JOHN PRITCHARD & CO.

in conjunction with Messrs.

GRANT STEVENSON & CO.

Will Offer for Sale by Auction
At the *STANLEY HALL, MACCLESFIELD*
On Tuesday, Wednesday, Thursday and Friday, 11th—14th October, 1938
commencing at 1.30 p.m. each day.

Solicitors: Messrs. STEPHENSON, HARWOOD & TATHAM, 16, Old Broad Street, E.C.2.
Auctioneers: { Messrs. GRANT STEVENSON & Co., 65, Holland Park, W.11.
{ Messrs. JOHN PRITCHARD & Co., Bank Chambers, Bangor, N. Wales.
Land Agent & Local Office: Mr. L. R. WILLIAMS, J.P., F.L.A.S. The Estate Office, Alderley
Park, Chelford, Cheshire.
Tel.: Alderley Edge 2303 and 3135.

Part Two

THE VILLAS

*"To do justice to the domestic architecture of
Alderley Edge much more ought to be known."*

*N Pevsner - Cheshire
(Buildings of England 1971)*

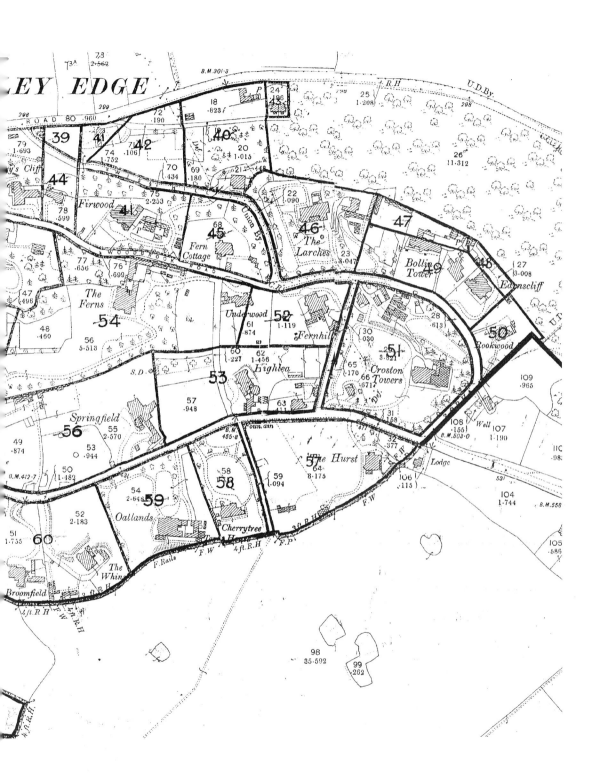

Alderley Cottage is shown here in its aboriginal form in an 1864 sketch by HT Gaddum.

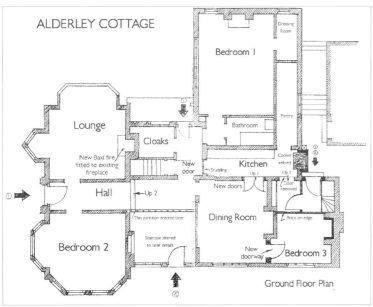

Plan of Alderley Cottage in its final form.
Courtesy Peter Adamson

THE VILLAS
A gazetteer of the villas on the hill

Every house tells a story. What started out as a study in architectural history has turned into social history. Architecture on this sort of level is but an expression in bricks and mortar of the lives that produced it.

What follows is part architectural and part social history, spiced with anecdote. The depth of the architectural detail and the selection of the stories is largely determined by luck and goodwill - another couple of years might produce a different story altogether.

Acresfield, see **Elmbank**.

Alderley Cottage, Congleton Road

Not originally a villa, not de Trafford property, nor even in Wilmslow/St Philip's parish. It stands at the tip of the puzzling Stanley 'tongue', on a rocky outcrop with a probable mine adit underneath, the spot marked by a rare old large yew. Now a trim villa, albeit partly in Cheshire cottage style; but an 1865 drawing by HT Gaddum shows an aboriginal timber-framed and thatched cottage. It was turned into a gentleman's residence in two stages. First a new crosswing c1870 see Oakwood. Then in about 1910 the old part rebuilt in replica, complete with the characteristic Stanley dormer. Minor fragments of old woodwork inside, possibly ex the Old Hall. It was one of the Massey's own houses, leased by Lord Stanley to Thos Callwood (eldest son of Isaac) and Ada Massey in 1895 for their lifetimes or 33 years at £15 pa.

Measured drawing of the 'cottage' part of Alderley Cottage as rebuilt in about 1910.

Alma Terrace

Pair of large 'Elizabethian' brick semis, tall and gaunt, at the bottom of Macclesfield Road. Alderley Edge High School for Girls founded in the two houses 1876 by Miss J Joyce. *"Education in Alderley Edge is provided for the ordinary children, in the school next to St Philip's church. Education of a higher order, is provided for the daughters and younger sons of the gentry by the High School." (Contemporary advert).* Extended 1884, possibly by Crowther. Became St Hilary's in 1913. 1955 became a Woodard school. 1957 acquired Westwood, 1962 Barnfield. 1977 Alma Terrace demolished but the 1884 extension remains. Due to amalgamate with Mount Carmel autumn 1999 and revert to the original name.

ALDERLEY EDGE HIGH SCHOOL
Alterations & Additions

Ashfield, Macclesfield Road. Now the Edge Hotel

Built c1850 for one of the Crewdson family. Of red ashlar - the stone came from a small quarry on site, remembered as 'the hollow' and now occupied by a house called Quarry House. Steep slate roof, dripmoulds over the windows making it mildly gothic or Elizabethian but internally it is very similar to Westwood and many others, eg stair with iron and plain wood balusters alternating.

From 1928-38 the "happy family home" of Mr Handasyde-Dick, cotton merchant at Wilson Latham of Whitworth Street Manchester. There were five in the family plus a Scottish nanny, "really part of the family", a cook, kitchen maid and housemaid all living in. Hacker the gardener lived on Moss Lane. (see p28) The family moved several times, always within Alderley Edge, according to their financial status and health.

1938 sold to Dr Mackessack who never moved in because of a hive of wild bees. Full of American Servicemen in the period leading up to D-day.

Now an hotel. The house has been turned round. The original entrance was on the west side, not facing the road as now, and is concealed by a large conservatory dining area. Big steel-framed bedroom wing added at the back 1998-9.

Barnfield, Congleton Road

Barnfield is on Stanley land on the Alderley Cottage 'tongue'. Evidently they decided that this odd bit of land might as well go for building even though they resisted any other residential development for so long. See also West View and Oakwood. Red brick Italianate villa with a disproportionately grand Ionic portico at the front in the finest stone, "all fur coat and no knickers", although this is not entirely fair because there are

Ionics in hallway as well. Stableyard to one side with a small water tower. 1920s Squash court built to rear with a glasshouse leaning to.
1962 St Hilary's Junior school.

Details of the St Hilary's extension to Alma Terrace.

68

Barnfield c1965, newly
acquired by St Hilary's.
Courtesy Jenny Youatt

Mr. J. H. A. Tipping, M.A.

Barnfield, showing the
covered yard and water
tower.

Barnfield front elevation

Barnfield side elevation; the service wing has three stories with no cellars, the family part two stories plus cellars.

70

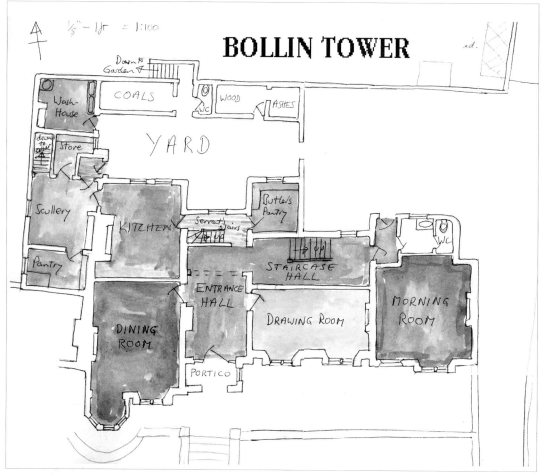

BOLLIN TOWER

COALS
WOOD
WC
ASHES
Down to Garden
Wash-House
YARD
Store
down to cellar
Scullery
Pantry
KITCHEN
Servants stairs
Butlers Pantry
STAIRCASE HALL
WC
ENTRANCE HALL
DINING ROOM
DRAWING ROOM
MORNING ROOM
PORTICO

Sketch plan of Bollin Tower as built. Note the large amount of space given to circulation, and to service quarters.

Mr. A. Hardy.

Far left: Detail of the tower shows the 'brid and babby' of the Stanleys.

Left: Mr Asa Hardy of Bollin Tower, 1896

Beaucliff, Macclesfield Road now with the rather cool name of **Frog Castle**.
The lane at the side is Duck Lane, after Mr Robert Duck of Norwood. Yellow brick Italianate built round a central toplit stair.

Beechfield

Italianate villa fronted with yellow brick, but cheaper red brick shows on the yard side backing on to Hazelcroft and at the back. Small nice redbrick stable. Remarkable cut-leaved beech tree shades the garden. (illustration p24)

Bishop's Lodge

Yellow brick Italianate house, symmetrical, relatively modest. Bought by the diocese for Gordon Strutt, bishop of Stockport. His successor got a modern house in Bramhall.

Bollin Tower, Woodbrook Road

A blackened stone tower with a smaller turret clinging to it rears above the trees, grim and mysterious, the perfect complement to the more sinister side of the Edge. Cruella de Vil's house indeed. There are two unequal square pele towers as well, and a kink to the west beyond which for many years there was an unfinished section possibly intended as a conservatory, marked 'ruin' on the map.

The earliest Directories list an Alderley Castle, Mr John Rogers architect. Surely this must be it, in which case it is the very first one *".... went over to Alderley Edge to look over a piece of land bought by Mr Rogers."* writes the de Trafford steward in his diary for 11th October 1843, the first such entry. *"........ no trees on it worth having"* he continues, *"to have Walton's house at valuation, excepting Sir Tho thinks fit to make him a present of it."* There must have been some sort of house on the site already, but evidently Sir Thomas de Trafford didn't think much of it. The name Castle is incidentally confirmed by the deeds.

The house was put up in 1844-5, along with The Gables next door, which shares the same romantic driveway. Bollin Tower's grim appearance is deceptive, for the back is smoothly rendered, facing an attractive setted court with small outbuildings and a pear tree, and the inside is quite innocuous. No flying staircases, no sweating walls, no flaring torches or suits of armour. Just a pleasant enough gentleman's residence with a couple of mildly gothic fireplaces. The house is actually built of red brick with a skin of rugged sandstone wrapped around the front. Disappointingly there is no sensible way up to the round tower, nor does it even have a floor, but it does command a fabulous view.

A puzzle :- prominent on the round tower is a carved representation of the Stanley 'Brid and Babby' or Eagle and Child. What is it doing there? Could it relate to some land exchanges between Stanley and de Trafford recorded by the de Trafford agent in 1845?

An unlikely owner was James Henry Sellars, architect and partner of Edgar Wood. He bought it in 1945 after army occupation and set up an office at the back in partnership with his son Norman. Mr Sellars was a progressive architect, a pioneer in the use of concrete for flat roofs and large areas of glass. Perhaps Bollin Tower was his secret, like Dorian Grey's portrait. In 1952 he divided the house into two, and now it is three.

Mr. J. Bowden.

J Bowden, Architect, Broad Ing

Brampton House, originally **Osborne House**

One of a group of three on Trafford Road (one has gone) of slightly lesser pretensions than the the majority of the villas. No back stair, only two main living rooms. Nevertheless it is an imposing house, of yellow brick, basically symmetrical with a central recess set off by some fancy ironwork. It looks as though the front door should be here, but it is set off to the side instead. Pretty little stable at the rear, and a back garden just, but only just, big enough for a tennis court. Tennis has been quite a craze in Alderley Edge.

Broad Ing, Beechfield Road

Built 1889 for Thomas Bouchier Moxon, banker and financier; architect J Bowdon, de Trafford agent, builders Isaac Massey & Sons. " .... *after so many years of strenuous work, involving so much responsibility, and the close study of abstruse questions relating to finance, currency, and the commerce of a great city like Manchester, well-earned and sweet is the rest he obtains in his beautiful home at Alderley, commanding as it does, some of the most extensive views across the great plain of Cheshire, the prospect extending on a clear day to the distant mountains of Wales."* (Manchester Faces & Places 6 1894)

Miss Phyllis Moxon his daughter lived on here alone *"more glass out than in, squirrels running in and out, veneer peeling off priceless antiques - she looked like a tramp herself when she came into the village but very generous to those in need"* (*Harold Smith*). She used to mow the lawn in the middle of the night, singing. House demolished so it only served the one family. Now 3 storey townhouses on the site. Just the gatepiers remain.

Broomfield, Macclesfield Road

Built 1845-7 by Thomas Worthington, then articled to Messrs Bowman and Crowther, for John Swanwick, with extensions after 1869. This was the 5th villa. Pale local sandstone with a heavy roof. First part is medieval or Puginian gothic, with mullions and an oriel, but the later parts, also by Worthington, are timber-framed with sash windows.

The house was the result of a good bit of networking, as we would say today. Swanwick, Bowman, Worthington, and possibly Crowther as well, were all linked by membership of the Cross St Unitarian church, one of the powerful non-conformist centres of Manchester.

Sometimes nicknamed 'the Mayor's nest' because of the way the (old) Town Hall was virtually an extension of it.

The story starts in Manchester with two gentlemen walking in to work from Cheetham Hill. John Swanwick, a stockbroker, mentioned to his young friend Thomas Worthington, who was training as an architect with Bowman and Crowther, that he had seen a plot of building land out at Alderley Edge, and heard of the splendid bribe of a free pass offered to house-builders there by the Railway Company.

The upshot was that Henry Bowman agreed to take the plot and build two houses upon it, one to be leased to Swanwick. Bowman designed The Whins himself but Broomfield he allowed his young apprentice to do.

So Broomfield was the first work in Thomas Worthington's long career as an architect. Its medieval gothic style, far from being old-fashioned, was the latest thing. The firebrand AWN Pugin had led the rebellion from 200 years of classicism by rediscovering the middle ages, so Broomfield, like Crowther's Redclyffe Grange, was something new as well as something old.

The machinations of fate determined that Worthington's involvement with Broomfield did not end with the handover to Swanwick. In 1869 the original lease came to an end, and the Swanwicks moved to Hale Barns. Worthington, now a successful architect, was able to buy the house himself from his former master. A dream come true, but sadly his wife Elizabeth died soon after the move, following the birth of their fifth child, Charles Welby.

In 1873 Worthington married again. His second bride was none other than Edith Emma

Swanwick, the first Swanwick child to be born at Broomfield and said to be the first cottontot baby of the Edge. She was 23 years his junior. She bore him six children, making eleven altogether.

Thomas died in 1909, full of years and as vigorous as ever until shortly before his death. For his full story read the excellent *'Thomas Worthington'* by Anthony Pass, 1988. Edith lived on at Broomfield until it was finally sold in the 1930s following her youngest son's marriage.

This house was for sale in 1999 at a million pounds, so it has perhaps squared in value. The sale particulars tell us that it was ..... *built for Sir Thomas Worthington in 1875* ...., which is three mistakes in seven words. Money doesn't buy you accuracy!

Cerin Amroth, Beechfield Road

Built 1972 for Michael and Helen Grindrod by Anthony Grimshaw of Wigan, architect. There are many infill houses on the Edge. This is just one example, included because it is eyecatching and interesting.

"'Behold! You are come to Cerin Amroth,' said Haldir. 'For this is the heart of the ancient realm as it was long ago, and here is the mound of Amroth, where in happier days his high house was built. Here ever bloom the winter flowers in the unfading grass: the yellow elanor, and the pale niphridel. Here we will stay a while ....*" (Lord of the Rings by JRR Tolkien).* The Edge might seem an appropriate place for the mound of Amroth, but the Grindrod's first house, also designed by Tony Grimshaw, was at Haigh near Wigan. It was called Lorien, the last friendly house in *'Lord of the Rings'.*

Cerin Amroth was built in the kitchen garden of **Acresfield** (once **Elmbank**), one of five different houses all by different architects. Work was delayed by a builders' strike and by the changeover from feet and inches to metric. It is a compact house almost square in its footprint but designed as a diamond. Single-pitched roof follows the slope of the hill and falls diagonally. Built of small square grey blocks (originally planned to be in yellow brick but Manchester had just bought the entire stock) with black paintwork. Silver runish letters for the house name set the tone.

The interior is planned diagonally across the square. A large single volume forms the living space and from it is divided off just 2 or 3 small rooms downstairs and two bedrooms and a small bathroom up an iron spiral stair in the top corner. Overall effect with contemporary furnishings and art is very good. The house is airconditioned, which is still quite novel in England.

Garage and greenhouse plus gazebo added in 1995. The gazebo, which gained several architectural awards, is perched in the top corner of the garden. Trapezoidal spaceframe fully glazed on two sides and braced by silver metal frame and wires. Really an office, it has a tiny washroom hidden in a freestanding teardrop-shaped turret in the centre. Independently air conditioned.

The garden carries on the geometry of the house to some extent. Large pond, steeply mounded lawns, veg patch. Two metal sculptures by Michael Kinsky - *'Doorkeeper'* and *'Wedding Invitation'*.

Cherrytree House, Macclesfield Road

1892 - so it is a late one - by George T Redmayne for Charles Railton and built by Isaac Massey. Shiny red brick with some timber-framing and tall sculpted chimneys. Mr Redmayne lived down the hill on Ryley's Lane. Extra land was acquired at the back from the Stanleys in 1904, bulging out from the original boundary; it is now built on.

A Railton Terraplane sports Saloon. Very light chassis with big engine. Result — 0-50 m.p.h. in 7⅓ secs. etc

The Railtons came to Alderley Edge in 1860 and lived in several different houses before building Cherrytree. Charles Railton wrote *'The Story of Alderley Edge and its Parish Church'*, an entertaining booklet in which he remembers his youth. Reid Railton, who belonged to the third generation, was an engineer specialising in the design of high speed cars and boats, which he sometime tested on Swiss Hill (not the boats!). In 1947 Cobb took the world land speed record at 400 mph in a Railton Special, but died in Railton's Crusader while attempting the record for water in 1952.

Cherrytree served as a billet early in World War 2 for the fifty soldiers of 'A' Troop, Royal Artillery 960 coastal defence regt. B and C troops were further down Macclesfield Road and HQ was in a large white house (?Hillside) almost at the bottom of the hill. Frank Hillier, of the Hillier's Nursery family, was among those in A Troop. He returned to Cherrytree in 1991 and this is taken from letters and newspaper cuttings at the time. They trained with old 15-pounder guns in the garden and paraded on the main road. The Institute served tea and eggs and beans on toast for 6d, but baths entailed a weekly march to Macclesfield.

The troop went on to Swansea then to the Middle East, Africa, Sicily, then the D-Day landings and finally the relief of Belsen. Not many of the Cherrytree 'pals' were left by then.

Croston Towers, Macclesfield Road

This house was demolished c1947 without a visual record, which is a pity. It was of rock-faced stone, like **Ferns** and **Bollin Tower**, big and castellated with more than one tower. The name Croston may refer to the de Trafford's Lancashire seat, the birthplace of Sir Thomas de Trafford, who started the development of Alderley Edge.

An Agnew house for a short time, but this extensive dynasty is more associated with Nether Alderley. The Schill's house in *'Manchester Made Them'*.

Gardener's cottage and the stable remain, as do traces of the once very fine garden.

Croston Cottage, Macclesfield Road

May be pre-railway because it does not conform to the standard de Trafford conditions - too close to the boundary. An older house turned into a villa, it faces down the hill.
Georgian proportions with gothic glazing bars.

Earnscliff, right at the top of **Woodbrook Road**

A big Italianate house now painted white. Short tunnel in front with an iron gate is, I suspect, nothing to do with mines or legends, but gives access to the house's water tank. The early houses all had their own arrangements for water.

A well-known resident for many years was Dr Heywood who practised at St John's Street in Manchester. He had one of the first cars but would not allow it to be used on Sunday, which necessitated three walks down the hill to St Philip's and back.

Elmbank, Beechfield Road

Large yellow brick house with red brick at the back where it doesn't show. In the 1890s the home of John Bernouin Rowcliffe who came from Tarporley; he built four very charming Arts and Crafts cottages there. His son William Edward moved to Ferns after the Hopkinsons left.

In 1919 extra land was leased from the Stanleys and the house was divided into two, now called **Acresfield** and **Half Acre** - the names are self-explanatory. Half Acre incorporates the splendid ballroom, a very characteristic addition to the original house with a raised dais in the curved bay for sitters-out; and a stable, now living accommodation, with pretty stencilled decoration in swags.

Ferns

Right in the centre of the villas, and central in importance because of the book *'Manchester Made Them'* by Katharine Chorley, 1950, which records so well the vanished life of the Edge.

Ferns has gone, replaced by a smaller but still classy house called **Franklyn**. She devotes a whole chapter to the old house so we can get an excellent picture of it. It was built of rusticated sandstone, with two gables on three sides but the fourth complicated by a kitchen yard, outbuildings and a big coach-house yard. Above the porch was a tower with a battlemented top, and there was another with a pitched roof - probably a water tower - between house and stableyard. The inside sounds like many another Alderley Edge villa. A dark and manly dining room, a bright and feminine drawing room and a slightly unloved billiard room all opening off a good hall and staircase. Underneath the stairs is the door to the service part of the house :- lower hall, big kitchen and sculleries, and steps down to the cellars and up to the attics.

Katharine Hopkinson, as she was, was born *'in the year of Queen Victoria's Jubilee'* - which must be 1897, eight years after her brother Campbell. Her father, Edward Hopkinson, was a brilliant electrical engineer and a managing director of Mather and Platt. He was also vice-chairman of a new firm, Chloride Electrical Storage. He was one of five brothers and five sisters; they were all clever. Her mother Marianne (Minnie) was an Irish protestant from County Antrim. Her Hopkinson grandparents had a house called Inglewood in Bowdon. They had moved out from Grove House, where the Whitworth Art Gallery is now, and before that the family house was at Ardwick Green - a typical progression.

Much can be learnt about life at Ferns by reading Katharine Chorley's book carefully. They had a housekeeper, Louisa, a parlourmaid who rather typically is not named, a cook, Rose, and a nanny or governess called Meme who is remembered with great fondness and was clearly one of the family. The servants' bedrooms were in the attics and they ate together in the big kitchen. Outside - Katharine Chorley devotes another chapter to the garden - there was the redoubtable Grundy, the gardener of whom the young Katharine was frightened, a coachman called Godfrey and a stableboy who is not named. The horse was called Paddy and they had a wagonette. Later they had a chauffeur who knew nothing about cars, called Richardson.

The original plot, largest of all at 5.5 acres, had been leased in 1845 to Benjamin Gibbons of Manchester, manufacturer. The 1851 census gives Howard Johnson, physician, 2 bath servants and 2 patients, so it sounds as though it was an embryonic Hydropathic establishment. Matlock built its prosperity on such establishments but they never took off here. The Hopkinsons came in about 1892, and Mrs Hopkinson died in 1936. There was only one other owner before it was demolished:- Edward Rowcliffe, solicitor, son of John Bernouin Rowcliffe of Elmbank.

The lodge (now Franklyn Lodge) remains on Macclesfield Road, at the head of a long winding drive. Very few of the villas ran to a lodge. It is an elaborate little building, cross-shaped with a porch, in Tudor gothic. The walls are of pinky sandstone but all the dressings are done in the tough yellow robinsfoot stone that crops up here and there on the Edge - except for a single lintel which was too long and had to be brought from Derbyshire.

Fern Cottage, Woodbrook Road

White roughcast house, not originally very big. A ballroom, designed by Fairhursts, was added in 1922 at a welcoming angle. The site was redeveloped in the 1990s with further dwellings disguised as a country house stableyard.

Fernhill, Woodbrook Road

Yellow brick with some stone trim; Italianate with round arches.

This was the retirement home of John Ramsbottom, Chief Mechanical Engineer of the LNWR, from 1880 until his death in 1897, aged 82. He started as an apprentice with the old Manchester and Birmingham Railway at their Longsight workshops. After retiring he remarried, took on consultancy of the L&Y Rly and helped design Horwich works.

Firs see Squirrel's Jump

Firwood, Woodbrook Road

By John Gregan for John Heugh, a wealthy Scottish merchant and shipper. Legend has it that Mr Heugh hoped to spy his shipping in the Mersey from the tower. He was a considerable collector of art; his collection, which was bought from Agnew's, included several Turners and 75 Roberts drawings. Gregan was Scots too, an excellent architect and originator with Edward Walters of the palazzo style for Manchester warehouses. Gregan's best is Heywood's bank now Royal Bank of Scotland opposite St Ann's church.

Firwood is an Italianate villa in yellow brick with round arches on some windows and pediments on others. Basically symmetrical but with a tall Osbourne-type tower placed asymmetrically. Shallow-pitched slate roofs.

In 1906 the Pilkingtons came to live here; they extended it considerably, and this was perhaps the best-known house and family on the Edge. The family firm was Clifton opencast colliery, five miles north of Manchester. A clay deposit had been discovered here accidentally in 1888. William Burton of Wedgwood's suggested tilemaking and in 1891 Pilkington's Tile and Pottery Company was formed under the chairmanship of Lawrence Pilkington. Still extant, it was an innovative company and produced, at intervals, some extremely beautiful things. (see Pilkington's Royal Lancastrian Pottery and Tiles by AJ Cross 1980)

The Pilkingtons are an old Lancashire family related to the de Traffords and bearing the same motto NOW THUS. Lawrence was a younger brother of the famous St Helen's glassmakers. He was a cultured man, published several slim volumes of verse and two historical novels based on life around the colliery. They were illustrated by his daughter Margaret; the other daughter was Dorothy. The Hopkinsons at Ferns were close friends and Margaret also illustrated a book called *'Hills and Highways'* by Katharine Chorley (Hopkinson). The friendship dated back to a climbing accident which left Lawrence Pilkington very lame and which is recounted in *'Manchester Made Them'*. A lift *'like the Ritz'* was installed at Firwood especially for him. He was also an organist, and Firwood sported a fine organ. Where is it now?

Margaret Pilkington was not someone you forgot. Small but formidable, she was a tremendous organiser and an accomplished artist, generous with her time and ready to use her money to further the things she believed in. Her memories, recorded for the Edge Association in 1972, complement those of Katharine Chorley as one of the most valuable documents of life in the villas.

Firwood in its glory days, from the garden.
Courtesy Phyllis Redding

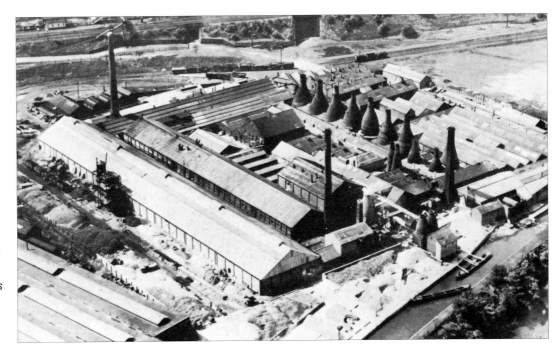

The Pilkington Tile Works at Clifton.
Courtesy Pilkington's

Far left: Pilkington family group in the window of Firwood.
Courtesy Phyllis Redding

Left: 80th birthday photograph of Margaret Pilkington.
Courtesy Rosemary Marsh

ROYAL LANCASTRIAN POTTERY
MANUFACTURED BY

ROYAL
P
TRADE MARK
LANCAST
RIAN

PILKINGTON'S TILE & POTTERY CO. LTD.,
CLIFTON JUNCTION, MANCHESTER

Courtesy Pilkington's

Nursery tiles designed
by Margaret Pilkington.
Courtesy Pilkington's

Firwood Cottage

The Gables

Hazelcroft; garden side.

Firwood Cottage

Stands below, on Mottram Road. A stylish little house and stable built of red brick with yellow brick dressings and a shallow-pitched stone roof, the windows deepset in groups under rounded arches.   Here lived the Leahs who were gardener/chauffeur and cook to the Pilkingtons. There were several heated glasshouses and an extensive kitchen garden in the lower part of the garden which was linked to the house, across Swiss Hill, by a romantic stepped path, luxuriant with mosses and ferns. The Pilkingtons employed five live-in servants and four or even five gardeners, but made a point of being not as lavish as the Crewdsons at Springfield.

Across Woodbrook Road was the Dell garden, really an old quarry which they had acquired from Ferns. The two sisters built a new house there and moved across in the 1970s. They took the name Firwood across with them, so the old house had to be renamed **The Cedars**. They disposed of their assets most munificently, giving the old Firwood to the University, Firwood Cottage to the Leahs, and a chunk of the Edge to us all, via the National Trust.

Frog Castle, see Beaucliff

The Gables, Woodbrook Road

First called **Sunnybank**. On the same parcel as Bollin Tower, served by the same narrow setted driveway cut right down into the bedrock, and built of the same heavy rock-faced stone. Could it be that it was intended as a gardener's house, or even as a dower house, to Bollin Tower? It was originally quite small but has been considerably extended - note how the stone colour changes. Although right at the top of the hill it shelters under a knoll, so commands no view over the plain.

Hazelcroft, Congleton Road

Built in about 1850 for Isaac Waithman Long and his wife Eliza. A large Italianate house of finest red brick with lavish stone dressings. Architect not known; it could perhaps be by Edward Walters.

The house is grander than most, impressive through and through, from the 4 feet wide front door to the built-in cupboards on the backstair. Even the cellars are magnificent. But it has posed a number of puzzles. As built, there was an extremely lavish open space for entertainment swirling about the big toplit stair, with open balconies above. There is, as usual,

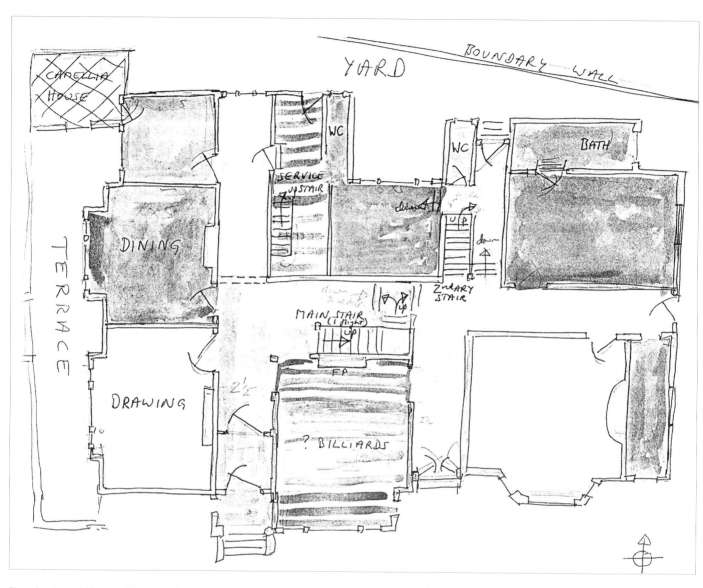

Sketch plan of Hazelcroft as built. A puzzling plan;
note the apparent superfluity of external doors
and staircases, and the huge circulation area which
includes the billiard room.

Sarah and Edward
Gaddum
Courtesy Anthony Gaddum

On the 13th inst. at Wilmslow Parish Church, by the Rev. J·
W. Consterdine, assisted by the Rev. J. Haden Cope, EDWARD
CHARLES GADDUM, second son of F. E. Gaddum, Esq. of
Adria House, Didsbury, to SARAH ELIZABETH, second
daughter of the late J. W. LONG, Esq. of Hazlecroft, Alderley
Edge.

Far right :Entrance Hall,
Hazelcroft
Right: Stairwell,
Hazelcroft

a backstair but there is also a third staircase. What was it for? Perhaps the house was designed to be run as two establishments by an extended family. Or perhaps it was to allow for independent family circulation while parties were in progress - or possibly both.

Hazelcroft is one of only two or three to have a lodge, although it is somewhat different in style and was built a little later than the main house. It never had a very big garden - just over two acres - but by pushing the house up hard against the boundary with just a narrow service yard adjoining Beechfield it was possible to incorporate an out-and-back drive, pleasure garden and kitchen garden, and a paddock with a small stable or even (see history) piggery. There was a camellia house. It probably fell into disuse during the first world war and was demolished afterwards, but the camellias flourish, now much bigger than their (unnecessary as it proved) shelter.

Mr Long was a Manchester merchant, said to be of Jewish European origin and to have anglicised his name. He did not live long to enjoy his new house - 1851 was his last appearance. His widow Eliza, only 41 in 1861, lived on there with her four daughters and five indoor servants until 1878 or 9. Sarah Long, the second daughter, married Edward Gaddum of St Mary's Cliffe in 1865.

In 1892 John and Peter Brownell are listed, adding some substance to the theory that it was a double house.

From the turn of century to the 1930s Hazelcroft's history is puzzling because the anecdotal evidence does not entirely square with the censuses and directories.

Edward Gaddum - sketched by H T Gaddum prior to his depature to Bombay Courtesy Anthony Gaddum

The story is that it was owned by Mr Simpson, pork butcher, originally Stimfig or some such name and another German immigrant, who served in the British navy in the first war. He kept a pig - and there the sty is in the corner of the garden on the 1909 OS map. In 1931 Amy Crossley lists Mrs CE Gilman and E Simpson both at the house so again the implication is that it was somehow divided. In 1924 a new garage was built by Massey's for William Gilman of Hazelcroft, Messrs Beaumont architects. In a common grave at St Mary's Alderley are William Gilman, 1929, Clara Elizabeth his wife, 1944, Walter son Lieut RAF, 1918, and Edmund and Elsie Simpson, 1953 and 1974. It is worth pursuing because the story goes that the Gilmans and/or Simpsons were Nazi sympathisers, blackshirts, and friends of Oswald

Mosley, and that there is a swastika in the hall floor underneath the fitted carpet. There are fasces in the plasterwork. We may note however that members of the family fought for the Allies in both great wars.

After the war Manchester City Council acquired it for a nursing home; eleven bungalows plus a warden's house were built in the grounds. The big house was used for entertainments such as bingo as well as residential. The house stood empty for a while, then was divided 1991 into three dwellings ("a commune for toffs" said one resident). The warden's house was demolished and two new houses occupy the site.

Highfield see **Trafford House**

Highlea
Yellow brick round-arch style villa on Underwood Road. Nice coachhouse with a cupola, now a separate dwelling.

Hillside Macclesfield Road
Angled away to catch the view. An early villa, white painted and smoothly stuccoed.
I think this was built for for Henry Winkworth, silk manufacturer and his wife Susanna, who moved out from Chorlton-on-Medlock in about 1850. But Mr Winkworth seems almost deliberately to have covered his tracks - his house is not named in either census nor in any of the contemporary directories - so it could have been another house very close by. This is annoying, as their younger daughter Catherine was a remarkable lady. She was a poet and translator of hymns; Nun Danket is the most famous - 'Now thank we all our God'. She had been tutored at home by William Gaskell and then James Martineau, both notable Manchester Unitarian divines, so she will have known Elizabeth Gaskell and Charlotte Bronte and Harriet Martineau - a redoubtable circle of friends. She was well-versed in German language and culture at a time when the royal family made this very fashionable, and spent a year in Dresden. Her 'Lyra Germanica', 1855 and 'Chorale Book for England', 1863 were best-sellers, rivalling 'Hymns Ancient and Modern' in their day. In 1862, following the collapse of the silk industry that followed from the free trade movement, the family moved away to Clifton in Bristol.

The Hollies, Woodbrook Road

An early one and very individual. Built in a shallow quarry, sheltered but with a fine outlook to the north. The original house was quite modest, roughcast, mildly gothic with iron 'estate cottage' windows and a stone roof. Extended in several campaigns, the original house becoming the service part and the original stairs the back staircase. Open hall with fireplace and stained glass including a delightful roundel of the Beacon. Cosy study, imposing drawing room.

Scattered remains of an elaborate iron pergola can be found around the garden. A bit of the ancient Edge vegetation clings on the rocks.

Coach house above, outside the quarry, now a separate dwelling.

Top: The Hollies: garden view.
Left: The Hollies: The Beacon, the Edge and an Armada galleon in stained glass.

Hollybank

On the corner of Macclesfield Road and Trafford Road but hidden by a high bank and two infill houses. A dramatic 'Elizabethian' house, roughcast, with very tall red star-shaped chimneys and scalloped gingerbread barge-boards. On the same parcel as Trafford House and sharing some architectural features.

Divided in 1937 - the other part was Greenbank - but made into one again in 1977 by Guy and Christine Milner, founders of the Edge Association.

The Hurst, Macclesfield Road

"Big white house, huge place. Full of Americans during the war" (Harry Smith).

Demolished and replaced by eight or nine new houses but the stable remains, and the lodge which was added on a little intake of Stanley land and the bowl of the main lawn. Dr Henry Wilde lived here for many years, until the Bellhouses took it in the 1930s. Dr Wilde was responsible for the *'This hill is dangerous'* and *'This hill is still dangerous'* signs, addressed especially to cyclists and originally featuring a skull and crossbones. He was the inventor of a searchlight which he would sometimes train on St Philip's steeple.

Ivy Cottage

On the main road in the village, diagonally opposite the de Trafford. Brick and timber-framing with a big gable at the front and a turret at the side. It incorporated, then was replaced by, garage premises, now in turn converted to the first of the cafe bars.

Lake Vale, now called **Osbourne House.** The name originally belonged to one of the yellow brick houses on the other side of Trafford Road; Mrs Hepworth found that it was easier to take the house name with her when she moved than change her address.

It stands in a quarry of the best building stone said to be that from which St Philip's was built, in which case it is unlikely to be earlier than 1856 since the quarry would have been active. And it does have a small lake. Roughcast with smooth quoins, like Trafford House next door. Puzzling in its layout and details, it appears to have had a very extensive makeover in about 1900. The prominent corner bay, cleverly angled out to catch the sun on this north-facing plot, is built of an early reinforced concrete, as is the porch, which seems ironic given the house's quarry site.

The Larches, Woodbrook Road

Primarily of interest for its garden. it was owned in the 1890s by William Peer Grimble Groves, a brewer of Regent Road Brewery, Salford. He was also a great gardener, landscaper and collector of orchids and a sponsor of plant-collecting expeditions, e.g. of Reginald Farrer and William Purdom to northwest China. His garden, one of the largest among the Alderley Edge villas at just over three acres, was written up in *'The Gardener's Chronicle'* for March 14 1896. The article lists approvingly the many choice conifers and rhododendrons growing well amongst the rocks underneath great beeches. It itemises the seven glasshouses. There was one attached to the house for palms, ferns, and flowering plants to be taken indoors as required. Another at the top of the hill was *'kept gay for knifing generally'* - not perhaps a phrase we would use today; we can take it to refer to cut flowers. There was a vinery and a peach house. And there were especially orchids, a mouthwatering list of species, all given the appropriate climatic conditions. *"The whole place is under the superintendance of Mr E Robertshaw, an old Trentham and Chatsworth man, under Stevens and Speed, and he certainly does every credit to the distinguished establishments in which he was trained."* What a treat these Alderley Edge gardens must have been in their prime.

Mr Groves left Alderley Edge in 1897, when he bought **Holehird**, a large estate between Windermere and Troutbeck. Mr Robertshaw went with him. The garden they developed there is now the headquarters of the Lake District Horticultural Society, open to the public and beautifully run. Mr Groves's handsome steam launch *'Kittiwake'* is preserved too, down at the steamboat museum. The sprawling house is now a Cheshire Home. Curiously enough it has earlier connections with Alderley Edge - see St. Mary's Cliffe.

The original Larches was demolished c1935 by Isaac Massey and replaced by a more convenient but still substantial house on the same site; three gables, lumpy grey pebbledash, metal windows, tiled roof; currently divided into two horizontally. What is left of the garden still very fine with tremendous rock-work and splendid trees, and the position is as stunning as ever - a carefully contrived effect of emerging from the rocky cutting of the drive to face the house on its flat plateau, and then become aware of the steep drop and vast panorama behind it.

The Lowlands

At the bottom of Macclesfield Road, overlooking the Methodist church. Unusual house built of banded brickwork with a Lake District slate roof and some timber-framing in the gables, one of which is set diagonally.

Maple Bank, see **Thorn Villa**

Norwood House, Macclesfield Road

Demolished in the early 1970s, having been used throughout the second war as clinic and canteen for evacuees, and then suffering the indignity of conversion to bedsits. It was a big white classical house with a portico in front and a curved bay on the west end.

Oakwood, Beechfield Road

This house does not properly belong here at all, despite being mixed in with the other villas and looking very much like them. It was built, along with West Bank and Barnfield, on land belonging to the Stanleys, in St Mary's parish and hence not strictly in Alderley Edge at all but in Alderley. It stands on the very odd and, I suspect, very ancient tongue of Stanley land coming down to Alderley Cottage, with visible boundaries to de Trafford land on both sides. A mine adit is supposed to run underneath from West Mine to Alderley Cottage.

Oakwood

Built in 1868 for R.Simpson Esq. The builder was Isaac Massey & Son and the architect E.Solomons Esq. Massey's are commonly supposed to have built Alderley Edge, but Oakwood - not by any means the earliest of the villas - is only the second on their list.

Edward Salomans (spellings vary) was a well-known and characterful Manchester architect and artist. He was a pupil of John Gregan, the architect of Firwood, and was one of the circle, along with AF Tait and Thomas Worthington, that produced Bowman and Crowther's great book *'Churches of the Middle Ages'*. His best-known building is the recently restored Reform Club on King Street in Manchester. His was the Spanish and Portuguese Synagogue on Cheetham Hill Manchester, now the Jewish Museum. He often carried out work for Agnews, the art dealers .and designed their showrooms in Liverpool and Bond Street London.

Oakwood is the most demonstratively High Victorian of all the villas. Built of hard red brick with ornamental texturing here and there, contrasting with plenty of stone dressings. The porch is virtually a separate structure of stone, with twirly columns and a shell in the pediment. The corner turret is even more elaborate, for the twisty columns have ivy trails carved upon them, and it has its own pointy roof with fishscale slates banded purple and green, topped by iron crown. The stair window too is all stone; it appears to be more refined than the rest. Upon it is carved, believe it or not, a very beautiful porcupine standing on a velvet cushion. The stone throughout is the red and cream blotched sandstone which can be seen in situ in the mines, used very smooth and closely jointed.

All the gables are shaped Dutch-style. Actually it is hard to give a polite name to the style of this house; it can only be called Victorian.

The inside has been hard to appreciate for some time, because unsympathetically divided. Outer porch led to a large inner hall with its own fireplace, lit by the stair oriel and by a rooflight via a rectangular well in the landing above; and also originally by a big side window of its own. Inner hall, stair and landing must once have been quite a spectacular composition.

The fittings are, or were, of superb quality but hideous design. The main stair had machine-carved wooden balusters, each one twisted with a central blob. The doors were glossily veneered in red and black woods, incorporating a central convex roundel as well as six rectangular panels. The rooms with the corner turret are very attractive and command fine views of the choice trees in the garden and the prospect towards Wales beyond.

The garden was indeed, and still is, splendid, in a very Alderley Edgeish, High Victorian way. All evergreens. There are big pines all along the boundary which probably pre-date the house. There is a monkey-puzzle, yews of different shapes, hollies of different colours, two types of cedar, some other conifers which I am hard-pressed to identify, and just one major deciduous tree, a red oak. Paths with stone edges run through beneath the understorey of rhododendron and laurel and it is altogether deliciously gloomy.

When it comes to its history Oakwood, as usual, poses a few problems. Because it was on Stanley land it appears in the Stanley Sale catalogue of 1938. The lease, however, is dated 25 Jany 1884, not 1868, and the leaseholder Spencer Henry Bickham, not Mr Simpson.

The story is that Mr Simpson was the Agent to the Stanley Estate and therefore the house and site were not leased but given to him. While Oakwood was a-building he was lodged at Alderley Cottage. But when Oakwood was finished he preferred to remain where he was. So he did, which explains the first phase of gentrification of Alderley Cottage. Instead Mr Bickham bought it for £3000.

It was a Hotel in the 1930s, requisitioned for American officers during the war, and a hotel again afterwards, but went into receivership in 1955. Bought and divided into 10 flats by Thomas Henry Bell. House and site completely revamped 1997-8 by Crosby Homes. 4 new houses tucked at the back so that the garden is substantially preserved, but the house was gutted. The top flat is the local residence of Alderley Edge's currently most celebrated couple, Posh 'n Becks.

Oakwood front elevation. A large Japanese Maple, recently felled, obscures part of the facade. The left-hand wing is an addition.

Oakwood front porch. Far right: Staircase oriel. The door below once led to a huge conservatory.

Far left: Oakwood landing window.
Left: bay window and a glimpse of the garden.

Oakwood: stone porcupine and cushion, beautifully carved on the stair oriel.

Edward Saloman's best-known building is the splendid Reform Club of 1870 in King Street, Manchester.

Mr. E. Salomons.

Site plan of Oakwood 1868 shows the complex boundaries hereabouts. A strange 'finger' of Stanley land points down to Alderley Cottage (not shown) on the other side of the main road. These boundaries are marked by ditches, suggesting considerable antiquity.

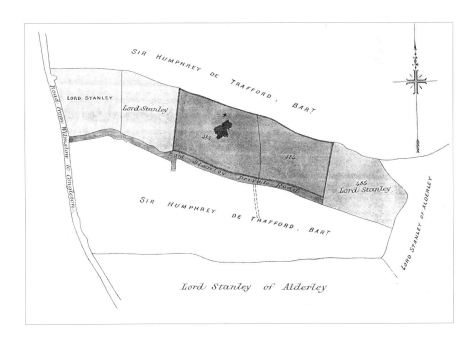

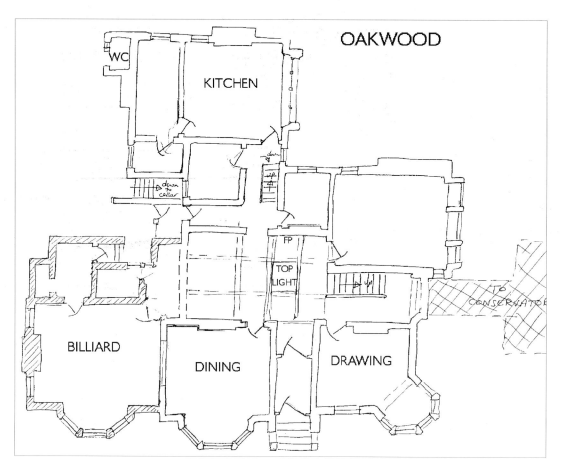

OAKWOOD

WC

KITCHEN

down to cellar

FP

TOP LIGHT

CONSERVATOR

BILLIARD

DINING

DRAWING

Sketch plan of Oakwood shows how a villa was zoned into family, circulation, and service areas. The billiard room wing is an addition.

Courtesy Crosby Homes

Oatlands, Macclesfield Road

This was a large square house built round a central glazed lightwell, with a lovely garden. William Ernest Pownall lived here from the 1930s with six live-in servants and two chauffeurs.

Demolished c1960 for eight new houses, including one called Oatlands and another, built over the old servant's gate cut in the rock like the one at St Mary's Cliffe, called Witches Gate.

Osbourne House see **Lake Vale** and **Brampton House**

Quinta architect FW Mee

Mr. F. W. Mee.

The Quinta, Beechfield Road

Built 1899 for E Ashworth; architect FW Mee, builder Isaac Massey.

Quinta :- a country-house or villa in Spain or Portugal; originally let at a rent of a fifth (Quinta parte) of the produce of the farm. (OED).

Large imposing house but with elements of cottage design beginning to appear. Pale red brick ground floor set off by a white roughcast upper storey with some timbering, and a long stone roof. Long sets of windows with leaded lights. Massey's were to become fond of using the local heavy stone slate for roofing, although it was already virtually unobtainable except as reclaimed material. Massey's agents would visit old farms in a wide area offering to re-roof them in modern materials in return for the stone slates.

In 1922 a ballroom was added for Mr Ashworth, with a beautiful sprung floor and an organ at one end, like Blackpool Tower ballroom, and a cellar was fitted out with a bar and brass portholes like a galleon. The pretty stable building, with a complicated Mackintosh-like wooden lantern, was made into a separate dwelling in 1997.

Ranfurley, Macclesfield Road

Tucked away in a grassy hollow. Gates say Westow Lodge, has been called Kilnfield which suggests industrial activity on the site. Rendered off-white, shallow slate roof, stained glass on stair. Garage/stable has glass porte-cochere.

Redclyffe Grange, Woodbrook Road

Built 1855 by Joseph Stretch Crowther for himself. Mr Crowther was just then building Alderley Edge school, having finished phase one of St Philip's church and shortly to begin phase two.

Redclyffe Grange is a charmer, a little showpiece, an architectural demonstration. *'This is how the gothic masons in the golden days of Merrie England would have built a house'*, runs the thinking behind it, *'if they had built houses like this'*. Which they didn't. England in the 13th century was far too dangerous a place, life was too short, the cities too small, for anything like a villa to exist - or a middle-class bourgeoisie for that matter. Such reasoning may sound far-fetched, but it was at the forefront of artistic fashion in the 1850s - just the time when Merrie England was in fact leading the world in the opposite direction, into a new world of technology and mechanisation; indeed just fourteen miles away was the very hub of the revolution. A curious state of affairs.

The name is more interesting than most. The novelist Charlotte Yonge achieved a huge success with *'The Heir of Redclyffe'* in 1853. I shall not easily forget my visit to Redclyffe four years ago. It was more like a scene in a romance than anything real. The fine old red sandstone house, crumbling away in the exposed parts; the arched gateway covered in ivy; the great quadrangle where the sun never shone, and full of echoes; the large hall, and black wainscotted rooms, which the candles never would light up. It is a fit place to be haunted.

Most modern readers, this one anyway, find the book impossibly slow and sanctimonious but it must have touched a chord. Part of the profits from it was devoted to fitting out the missionary schooner 'Southern Cross' for Bishop Selwyn. I wonder if every place called Redclyffe - there is one at Victoria Park and another at Barton - dates from exactly the same time.

The house is gothic through and through, from the tall castellated chimneys to the encaustic tiles on the hall floor. The roofs are very steep, with a gargoyle at the valley. Even the cast-iron drainpipe hoppers are gothic - now there's an anachronism. The windows are stone mullioned, some with tracery. The front door is a splendid piece, double-leaved, heavily framed, iron-bound, with a huge lock and key and a nice carved squirrel in the tympanum above it. The interior is planned on picturesque principles, with long internal views framed by pointed arches. Both sets of stairs are gothic and so are the fireplaces. Windows in the principal rooms are deeply set in pointed recesses complete with carved paterae. Doors and panelling are a strange compromise between the gothic ideal and standard 19th century joinery. It is not gloomy, as it may sound, but a cheerful house and so carefully thought out as to give endless pleasure.

The materials are interesting because they anticipate Arts and Crafts ideals. Instead of the custard brick of so many Alderley Edge houses or the hard red bricks of Manchester, Crowther has used soft local hand-made red bricks; in fact he has demonstrated their use by employing an unusual header bond. Instead of tiles or Welsh slate on the roofs he has used heavy Kerridge stone slabs, beautifully graded. The stone parts though, a trifle disappointingly, appear to be Bath stone. At least that gives the lie to rumours that he might have used spare stone from the church.

The garden is horizontal at the front and almost vertical at the back, in fact it incorporates a massive overhang, commanding a wonderful view over the plain. Linking the two is an arched gate guarded by carved stone dragons and a lizard. More assorted dragons once guarded the steep path down to Swiss Hill.

The history of the house as revealed by the deeds is complicated. Land was first leased in 1845 by Thomas Joseph de Trafford to W Lewis. On the 25th April 1855 it was divided into two and let by Sir Humphrey de Trafford and John Kay Farnworth to John Heugh of Firwood, then the next day the smaller one was underleased to JS Crowther. Mr Lewis and Mr Farnworth bought up a lot of land in the early days. The ground rent was £12-10s-0d to be paid in two installments. The exact date of the building of the house is never made clear. The 1861 census shows :-

Joseph S. Crowther	38	architect	Warwicks Coventry
Martha do. mother	67	landed proprietress	do.
Elizabeth Lawton servant	37	nurse	Liverpool
Harriet do. do.	16	Housemaid	Clitheroe
Jaye? Nugent servant	37	House servant	Carlisle

So Redclyffe Grange is a bachelor pad. It is strange that Mr Crowther appears to have lied about his age. He was actually 41.

Thomas Higson was here in 1878, and Louis Herbert Marriott in 1892. Mr Crowther had moved on to **Endsleigh** on Brook Lane. But evidently he retained ownership of Redclyffe Grange, for it was not until after his death in 1893 that it was sold, to Joseph Lindley of Didsbury, manufacturer.

Down below on Mottram Road is a pretty stable and cottage called Redclyffe Cottage, but it is in the wrong place. It originally belonged to Swiss Villa, but by some jiggery-pokery with the title deeds it became attached to Redclyffe Grange by Mr Lindley. It would always have been difficult to get a horse and carriage up to the house.

Edward S. Chesney, solicitor to the Bishop of Manchester, appears in directories for 1906, 1910, 1914 and is given a description in 'Manchester Made Them'. His son Denis was a regular soldier in India. He added an extension 1907 in a complimentary style, making it more of a family home.

Today it is still in single family occupation, and much loved, although it has lost the bottom of the garden. Nosy parkers walking past up Woodbrook Road may be puzzled by the chunks of gothic masonry in the garden. These were salvaged from the lost Crowther church of St Alban's Cheetwood in 1998.

The Ridge, Beechfield Road

Mr Tulloch's house in *'Manchester Made Them'*. They were the ones who served up dessert on gold plates. The house was only built in 1899 by Massey's, to designs by J Bowden, the de Trafford agent. The Ridge has an important place in the history of the area because it was an early toe-hold of ICI, used by them as a factory during the war, and then for hospitality. ICI, later Zeneca and now AstraZeneca, have dominated the area since they bought Alderley Park in 1955 for £55,000.

It was demolished in the 1960s to be replaced by two big ranch-type bungalows, swanky but cheaply built. These have been demolished in their turn for a development of five mini-manors.

A strange relic, recently needlessly destroyed, was this ornate gaslamp which had been partly engulfed by a lime tree. It stood on the footpath by the entrance to the Ridge site.

Rockside, Macclesfield Road

Yellow brick villa with a small red brick stable tucked in at the side, the two joined by a glass roof.

Rookwood, Woodbrook Road

Demolished c1968 to be replaced by three substantial houses, one of which has kept the name.

St Hilary's School see **Alma Terrace, Hurst Lea, Westwood** and **Barnfield.**

St Mary's Cottage and Swiss Hill.

St Mary's Cliffe, Woodbrook Road

Built about 1851 for JR Lingard, possibly by JS Crowther. From 1854 Mr Lingard also owned Holehird near Windermere, which has later connections with The Larches.

St Mary's Cliffe was demolished after a fire in 1971 but it is still worth a good account. Most of the villas were quite bland in their architecture. St Mary's Cliffe was not bland. It was the most spooky house on the Edge, all turrets and tall chimneys, overhanging porches and oriels, stained glass and huge gothic fireplaces. It was big too, and perched on its red cliffe amongst the pines made an extraordinary silhouette. I regret its passing, especially as the house which has taken its place, Jaysholme, is blandness personified.

From the drawings and photographs that chance has supplied it is possible to work out quite a lot about the house, but it is all very tantalising. It was a long T-shaped building with the downstroke, containing the service quarters, running up the hill parallel with Woodbrook Road. The cross-piece ran right to the cliff edge, with a gothic bay window hanging over it. In the angle between the two was a turret with a tall spire roof, probably lighting the stairs.

The house was of local red brick, with a diaper pattern of diagonals made in contrasting blue-ended header bricks. The roofs were tiled, with diapers as well, and had fancy cresting. There was a big two-storey porch of timber-framing, like the one in the courtyard at Adlington Hall. It carried a Tudor-style inscription above the great door:-
GODS:PROVIDENCE:IS:MINE:INHERITANCE.

- a picturesque whim, a serious statement by a puritanical Mancunian? What is interesting to an architectural historian is that Gods Providence House of 1652 in Watergate Street, Chester, was given a major rebuild in 1862. Could it be that timbers, even the inscription, of the old Gods Providence House ended up here? The architect for the Chester restoration was James Harrison - "the other Harrison" to distinguish him from the more famous architect of Chester Castle and Grosvenor Bridge. He designed St Margaret's, Whalley Range, and there is a suggestion that he might have worked with Thomas Worthington for a while.

Strangely enough the inscription itself survives, the only significant bit of St Mary's Cliffe to do so. Someone picked it up after the fire and propped it up in the outside toilet of a neighbouring house.

Now to the inhabitants of this extraordinary house.

The first was John Rowson or Rawson (both names appear) Lingard. Lingards and Rowson/Rawsons are common enough to make placing him difficult. They seem to have originated in Heaton Norris, Stockport and several acted as solicitors or agents to canal and railway companies. Was Mr Lingard solicitor to the M&B? His brother RBM Lingard-Monk (he added the Monk) was a prominent company solicitor, lived in Fulshaw Hall. John R Lingard is listed in Windermere directories as *of Holehird and St Mary's Cliffe, Chorley*. It seems strange that he should hold both houses but this may tie up with his railway business.

He was a big supporter of the building of the church at both places. At Holehird is a huge gothic fireplace that appears to be identical to one that existed at St Mary's Cliffe. A typical Crowther design, and I remind myself that Crowther too had a house in both places.

He died in 1856. Next came Edward Gaddum (1837-93), the second son of EC Gaddum of Adria in Didsbury; that house has gone too but is remembered in several street names. The Gaddums, a central European family, came to Manchester in 1826. They maintained their business interests in Italy and Switzerland all through the 19th century. Edward's brother Henry Theodore was a prolific sketcher, illustrating all aspects of the family's life and travels. He drew St Mary's Cliffe in 1864; it is very interesting that he labelled it *'alias awful cottage'*. Words like awful, awesome, tend to get downgraded in their meaning, but evidently even then it was considered spooky.

St Mary's Cliffe in a drawing by HT Gaddum of 1864. Note his caption. A further gabled extension was added to the right after this drawing was made. *Courtesy Anthony Gaddum*

On the 13th April 1865 Edward married Sara Elizabeth Long of Hazelcroft, see p87. Their initials were inscribed as monogrammes on each side of the great gothic fireplace at St Mary's Cliffe. She is supposed to have brought madness into the family.

Next came John Edward Lees, solicitor, who features in *'Manchester Made Them'*, followed by Peter Ermen. Evacuees from the Channel Islands and American soldiers are both reported here during the last war; possibly not simultaneously.

In 1960 it was the residence of the evil Selina Place, alias the Morrigan, in Alan Garner's *'The Weirdstone of Brisingamen'*. A more appropriate dwelling could not be imagined.

Finally in 1971, full of dry rot, it burned out most spectacularly and was demolished soon afterwards.

What is left of St Mary's Cliffe is the fine retaining wall on Woodbrook Road, partly sunk in the bedrock and with a 'witches gate' cut out of it; the house platform with the rock garden falling vertiginously below it, and two cottages below on the Mottram Road. Each is a pale reflection of the vanished mother-house. The stable house, Woodland Cottage, has been whitewashed and has lost its tall chimney. St Mary's Cottage, with mullioned windows and some timbering, stands on a little triangle cut off from the rectangular parcel by Swiss Hill. It has a surprisingly complicated history. It must once have been very tiny, a little gardener's bothy. At some stage it was enlarged to make two cottages at right angles to each other, each with a pretty wooden porch. Now it is back as one house and occupied by a senior professor at the university. Such is the value of a house on the Edge that on the neighbouring plot, a little patch of kitchen garden of unfavourable aspect, was being built the latest villa - a house of no small pretensions - as writing was in progress.

View of St Mary's Alderley.

Courtesy Anthony Gaddum

A splendid wedding photograph taken on 17th April 1912 on the cricket field, Moss Lane. The bride and groom are Ethel Twigg and Ernest Kennerley. Readers may be able to spot the bride's father John Twigg who also appears on pages 24 and 124, and John Edwin Twigg the headmaster of the village school. In the background loom the silhouettes of Redclyffe Grange and St Mary's Cliffe.

Courtesy George Twigg

Postcard view c1904 from the same spot shows the vanished Swiss Cottage in the centre. On the far right is the tower of Firwood and on the left are the houses on Squirrel's Jump.

Courtesy Jackie Stone

Alderley Edge   Dutton's Series

Sharston, Beechfield Road

A very late arrival, but did not last long in its first form. It was a flat-roofed, streamlined house of 1960s vintage built for one of the Simon engineering brothers. Today an enclave of bizarre villas by Rod Hackney and his team, each incorporating salvaged demolition materials.

Springfield, Macclesfield Road

Probably the grandest of the lot. It was built before 1850 on a splendid site, of a fine pinkish ashlar stone; the service wing was in a shallow quarry. The house had a tall French-style roof. It was surrounded by a couple of acres of parkland dotted with specimen trees, with a paddock at the bottom and the kitchen garden and greenhouses tucked in at one side. House and garden are considerably reduced today, though still impressive. This was Alfred Crewdson's house. The Crewdsons were in cotton, and were Quakers like the Waterhouses to whom they were related.

Squirrel's Jump

The name of a short unadopted track leading up to the Edge off Mottram Road. It need hardly be said that the name isn't as old as the road, but goes with the group of Spanish-style villas built in the garden of Swiss Lodge. The Firs and Wood Hill, however, date back to 1868. They are an anomaly amongst the villas, a pair of ordinary Victorian semis, built as boarding houses, made extraordinary by their position on the steepest slope of the Edge so that they have a full two floors below front door level.

Swiss Cottage, on Swiss Hill

It has gone, depriving us of one of the most characteristic landmarks in the Alderley Edge landscape. This was once a lovely house with a lovely garden, but it slowly deteriorated, losing its stable to Redclyffe Grange in 1893, the bottom of its garden to Spanish style villas on Squirrel's jump in the late 1950s, part of its balcony in the late 1960s, leading to final demolition in the late 1970s.

It was built on a very steep and difficult site, incorporating an old quarry face, on the north face of the Edge. It was indeed a Swiss chalet, with very wide eaves and tiers of green-painted wooden balconies, though the effect was somewhat marred by the yellow brick carcass. Stone steps zig-zagged steeply down to the stable on Mottram Road. A dull block of town houses occupies the site of Swiss Cottage today.

Thornfield, Macclesfield Road

Yellow brick Italianate with a slate roof. Additions were made in 1892 for TF Hamilton by George Redmayne.

Used as a factory during the second war while the owners lived in the basement, and then badly affected by dry rot, Thornfield was demolished in November 1969. Derek Cobb, architect, who built four new houses on the site, made a very dramatic watercolour sketch of the old house in its last moments.

Thorn Villa, Macclesfield Road; now called Maple Bank

A nice house, roughcast in a pinkish colour with smooth quoins. Mildly gothic in its detailing, like Hollybank and Trafford House. Part of an old cottage is incorporated at the back.

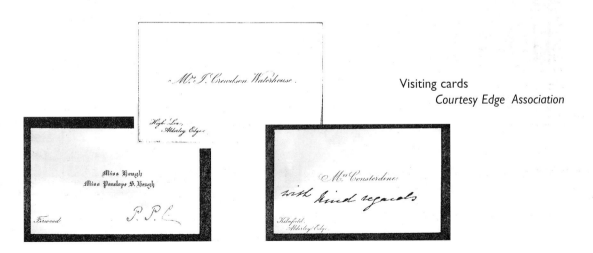

Visiting cards
Courtesy Edge Association

Trafford House, pair with **Highfield**

First deed 29 September 1845, a big parcel subsequently divided into five for houses which were built in the next few years. Roughcast and colourwashed, mildly Elizabethian. There are a number of house on the lower slopes, all built in this style and all associated with the earliest developers, Benjamin Gibbons and John Kay Farnworth. Like Brampton House, which has many similarities, this falls into a slightly more modest category than most of the villas, with no back stair and two, not three, main living rooms. Big enough to be pretty grand by modern standards, but small enough to have escaped division of the house or the garden. There is a pretty stable building in a hollow in front, which has had a fine billiard room added to it. One can just imagine the gentlemen after dinner crossing the few yards of darkness from the front door, taking a moment to enjoy their cigars and the stars, before settling down to a game, with the big green table a brightly gaslit island in the cosy wood-lined and firelit room. The garden commands a surprisingly fine prospect, although it is on the lowest slope of the Edge. A well by the front door may ante-date the house.

Underwood, Woodbrook Road

A distinctive house of reddish brick laid in a header bond contrasting with yellow brick quoins. The windows are deepset, grouped in twos and threes and fours with round arches, and there is a Rapunzel-type turret at the back. Very reminiscent of Firwood Cottage except for the big enveloping roof, which may be an alteration; in which case one can guess another Gregan house, like Firwood itself.

It was the Bles's house in *"Manchester Made Them"*. They were of Dutch Jewish origin.

Mr. M. S. Bles, J.P.

Underwood, the home of
Mr Bles in *'Manchester
Made Them'*, front and
back views.

West Bank, Beechfield Road

On Stanley land. Herman Zill 1906, Mrs Zill 1910 to 1934 then Miss Z. The Zills came from Dresden, where there are many villas of just the same type; especially reminiscent of Alderley Edge are those nestling in dense greenery on the steep bank of the Elbe. Although the centre of Dresden was almost destroyed in 1945 the villa suburbs are well preserved. Demolished and replaced by 14 nondescript houses, anywheresville, in a close of the same name. This development was a rallying point of the Edge Association.

Westwood, Congleton Road

Trim white stucco villa, nearly symmetrical and demure under its pyramid roof. Small stable. The upper floor was extended over to join the stable when a large nursery suite was added.

Bought in 1957 by St Hilary's as the senior school. Large school hall added at the back but the house itself is not greatly altered, retaining for instance a good butler's pantry with ranges of wooden cupboards and a full height built-in safe.

Mr. W. Tipping.

Westwood with the strange wooden shelter (was it for bicycles?) that disfigured the front for many years. The vanished conservatory is just visible.

Courtesy Jenny Youatt

The sketch plan shows an eminently typical villa even to its orientation.
The stable was originally detached.

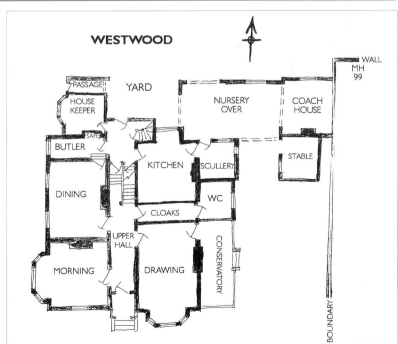

WESTWOOD

The Whins, Macclesfield Road

Built by Henry Bowman, as developer and architect, on the same plot as Broomfield. A yellow brick classical villa with a Doric columned porch, but unusual in its detailing. The way the structure is exhibited around the windows and doors indicates a man who is taking on board the preachings of Pugin even though he is still working in the classical mode.

Woodbrook

One of the first, listed in 1850. It was a pretty villa with twin gables overlooking the western prospect, contrasting in its trimness with the wild exuberance of St Mary's Cliffe. It stood in exceptionally fine grounds, even for Alderley Edge, and made the most of them, with a long drive winding up from Trafford Road.

In 1906 alterations and additions were made to Woodbrook by Isaac Massey & Co for A Heyworth Esq. The architect was C F A Voysey, one of the few top flight architects to make an appearance at Alderley Edge. The additions were made partly in yellow brick, which is uncharacteristic of Voysey, but with his typical flush-moulded windows and simple but beautiful joinery and ironwork, Voysey's work always looks more modern than it is. This is because he was so much copied in later years, not least by Massey's once the Stanleys started to develop their estate. Woodbrook, though, has not been lovingly cared for in recent years.

Woodlands, Alderley/Congleton Road

One of a pair of large yellow-brick semis with a splendid prospect
to the west over the Cheshire plain. Here lived for many years
Mr Hutton who is briefly remembered by Catherine Chorley
as a great fisherman. His daughter Emily was a heroine of
the First World War; she ran the field hospital at
Brookdale, was awarded the OBE, but died
soon after in 1919.

Wood Hill, see The Firs

Mr. J. A. Hutton.

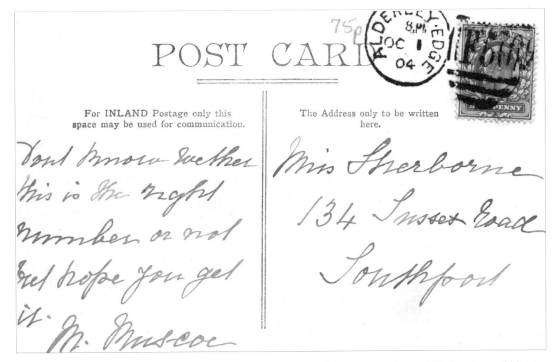

Reverse of the postcard on p119. Readers of Maisie
Mosco's books will find the sender's name curious.

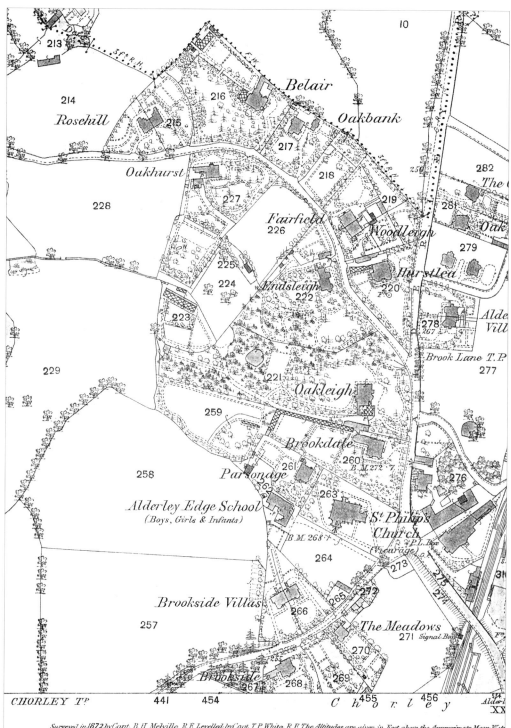

Surveyed in 1872 by Capt. B.H. Melville R.E. Levelled by Capt. T.P. White R.E. The Altitudes are given in Feet above the Approximate Mean V.ste

Zincographed under the Superintendence of Lt. Col. Parsons R.E. F.R.S. at the ORDNANCE SURVEY OFFICE, SOU

A GAZETTEER OF THE VILLAS BY THE STATION

As well as the villas up the hill there is a distinct group immediately to the north of the station. The Brook Lane ones are listed topographically rather than alphabetically:- starting at St Philips and going down the left side; then returning on the other side.

Brookdale

Built 1850s for James Jardine. Large yellow brick house with mottled local stone dressings. Big double-columned porch, bay set diagonally on the southeast corner. 1.7 acre ornamental garden with a very long greenhouse along the south wall.

James Jardine's story is told in *'Manchester Faces & Places'* Vol IV, 1892-3. He was the 'architect of his own future', a real Manchester Man. Born 1818 in the Irwell valley, he started as a clerk at Christy & Son, Fairfield and rose to be manager. Junior partner in Messrs Hugh Shaw and Co, fine spinners of Ancoats; rose to be head of the business now called Shaw, Jardine & Co, the largest fine spinning and doubling in Manchester.

Mr Jardine never forgot his humble start in life, and became a serious philanthropist as soon as he had the means to do so. Generous benefactor to Ancoats hospital - a new wing for sick children was built and endowed by him in 1888 at the cost of £13,000. On the board of Owens College, Chairman of Royal Exchange, Vice President of Salford Savings Bank. The new south porch of the cathedral, part of the major restoration by J S Crowther, was entirely at his own expense, as is recorded by a prominent inscription thereupon. He gave the east window of St Ann's, by the pre-Raphaelite Frederick Shields, in memory of Bishop Fraser. James Jardine was given the freedom of Manchester in 1890. He died at Brookdale in 1893, eleven years before his wife Hannah. Their son James Arthur had died in Eastbourne aged only 29.

Across the A34 was another parcel of land owned by Mr Jardine. Here Massey's built for him in 1874 a substantial coachman's house and gardener's house in a tricksy timber-framing, similar to the Trafford Arms, and a big block of stabling with a tower. This was all too big for private use - I think it was a business, horses for hire. With the motor age it became the Tower Garage, and is still so known although Higham's demolished the tower and the two houses in 1992 for no reason other than to save trouble.

Brookdale was an auxiliary Field Hospital in World War 1 - see pavement inscription at

The grand entrance portico of Brookdale with its fine monoliths - but what sort of order is this? - of Alderley stone. See the aerial photo on p8 for the whole house.

Cottages attached to Brookdale but across the main road, later part of Tower Garage, under demolition in 1994.

Tower Garage c1920
Courtesy S Higham

Tower Garage - a more recent view. The tower was demolished with the cottages in 1994, but the name lingers on.

Mr Jardine of Brookdale could have been the model for this life-like stone head in St Philip's - or was it Alfred Waterhouse?

the war memorial and the section on wartime.

Mount Carmel School, bought it in 1944, replacing the servants' wing with a large school building in 1955. Faced with rot in the roof they decapitated the entire house in 1972, rebuilding the upper floor with a flat roof. So there is not a lot left of Brookdale.

Oakleigh from the garden. See also the picture on p50.

Oakleigh

Demolished while this book was in preparation, August 1999. A plain house roughcast in grey though with quite a jolly wooden porch. Good stair at right angles with iron and wooden balusters alternating, a common feature, but otherwise rather plain and institutionalised. Big garden reasonably well preserved with an exceptionally fine weeping lime. A large conservatory was lost when British Railways blew up the railway bridge as part of the electrification programme.

Here lived Frederick Mehl, born Neider Walluf 1831, died Alderley Edge 1908. 'Auf Wiedersehen' says his memorial at the cemetery.

Mr John Twigg was the Mehl's gardener. He lived in a very plain cottage right at the bottom of the huge garden. Mr Twigg was much involved in local garden societies, and the Twigg family were great photographers of each other. His children used to cut through the parsonage garden to get to school where a nephew, John Edwin, was to became a well-known headmaster.

In 1945 Oakleigh was bought by Mount Carmel school as a boarding house. For a while it was the convent, and finally the Sixth Form Centre before its final demise.

124

John Twigg and his chrysanthemums at Oakleigh c1905.
Mr Twigg is the unwitting star of this book, appearing no less than three times.
Courtesy George Twigg

The gardener's cottage at Oakleigh, which was right at the bottom of the plot, c1938.
Courtesy George Twigg

The staircase at Oakleigh
is illustrated here
because it is no more
(see p50). Typically
spacious, toplit, with iron
and wooden balusters
alternating.

The uncompromising
facade of Endsleigh from
the lane. Note the way
its inside can be read
from the outside ; the
windows show where
the stairs are and their
relative sizes indicate the
size and importance of
the room within.

Endsleigh

Endsleigh - the garden front.

The villas are pretty standard in plan; usually double-fronted and two principle rooms deep, ie. roughly a square - a double pile. But not this one. It appears very big from the road, because the principal rooms are all stretched out in a row, but it is only one room deep. It is in a strange style too, a sort of institutional gothic, like an orphanage, although the garden side is more friendly. All this points to an architect with a strong personality. The list of works by Alfred Waterhouse (Cunningham and Waterhouse 1992) includes the following:-

1862 Alderley Edge Cheshire

House offices and stable

Client WW Hoyland

Contractors J Harwood; Ironwork W Young; Tiling T Oakden.

Cost £1,940

Waterhouse was undoubtedly a great architect, but he was better at town halls than private houses. Mr Hoyland did not stop here long, moving to Westwood on the Congleton Road, a conventionally pretty house.

Endsleigh was soon home to another architect, J S Crowther. He moved here from his own delightful Redclyffe Grange in the 1870s, although he seems to have lived away for a while in between times. It was his home until he died in 1893, at Southport, in the arms of his very young wife Richanda. She had been his housekeeper at Endsleigh, a not uncommon scenario in Victorian times. She inherited both houses plus a respectable fortune, but forfeited most of it when she married her childhood sweetheart Harry Hulme of Lowestoft in 1894.

A branch of the Crewdson family lived here in the 1930s. The Crewdsons had a large household. There was - most unusually - a butler, Mr Williamson *"bored out of his mind"*, who lived in the village. The cook *"always cross"* was Mrs Redhead, the housemaids Elsie and Gwen, parlourmaid Agnes and the kitchenmaid, who was bottom of the pile, Lois. There was a servants' hall at the back of the house and a proper bathroom - a major attraction to one brought up in a tiny cottage - for the servants. There were three gardeners, Leah (a local name) and his two sons, and a chauffeur, Jack Ward, who lived above the coach-house. The Crewdsons had two daughters, Joan and Barbara. And two huge dogs - Spondy and Tago. Their brother Theodore was killed in the War.

The staircase at Endsleigh is as unusual as the rest of the house with its arches and its fretted, almost Chinese, balustrade.

Oakhurst

A plain but good quality redbrick house with stone dressings, like Hazelcroft, and like Hazelcroft it was equipped from new with a form of warm-air central heating. A long nursery wing stretched out from the main block wing to the west, but was considerably reduced when the road was widened; a small stable building behind it.

Oakhurst has had very few owners. It was built for Hugh and Lydia Roberts after their marriage in 1850. They were Welsh Calvinists, but became heavily involved with St Philip's. There were four children of whom two, Lloyd and Bowen, were said to be mentally weak - their parents were first cousins. They had three maids Lucy, Mary and Celia, who wore starched caps and aprons, and two gardeners, Leah and Wood. Hugh's brother, John Foulkes Roberts, was Mayor of Manchester, his daughter Mary an unpopular Lady Mayoress because of her very strong views on Temperance.

The family business was Messrs JF & H Roberts cotton spinners. They had mills at Oxenhope, above Hebden Bridge, and at Foulridge, near Colne, and a warehouse at 21 Portland Street. All that is left of the firm today is the trade name Dormer.

Their unmarried daughter, also Lydia, looked after them until they died, giving up her

Lydia and Hugh Roberts of Oakhurst in 1910. The firm's coloured letterhead is shown below and contemporary photographs of one of the mills appear on pp 30 and 31.   *Courtesy Anthony Gaddum*

dearest wish to be a missionary; she died in 1940, still at Oakhurst.

British soldiers were then billeted here, the multiple showers put up for them in the cellar remain. The rooms were all numbered; they went up to 38.

The house was not sold until 1947, ending nigh on a century in the same family. It was the home of the Pinningtons for forty years and is only now in its third ownership.

Now returning ....

Rose Hill and Brookhill

Pair of large yellow brick semis.

Bel Air

Here lived for a while, with two nurses, Fabia, 'widow' of Henry Lord Stanley who died in 1903. Immensely fat, she was dislodged from Alderley Park with some difficulty by the family. Demolished; now a large new nursing home on the site. Some trees remain and a small rustic summerhouse.

Oak Bank

Plain grey roughcast house hidden in deep shrubbery.

Fairfield and Brooklands

A pair of large white stuccoed semis built before 1850; originally called 1 and 2 Brook Villas. In Brooklands lived John Earwaker, father of the famous antiquarian and dedicatee of his son's *'East Cheshire'* 1877. Most of the neighbours subscribed to it.

In Fairfield lived Thomas Satterthwaite, a Quaker and cotton king. His family originated on the shores of Windermere, looking northwards to the Fell called Fairfield. He is buried under an unadorned gravestone by the Friends' House in Wilmslow. The Satterthwaites built the College, derelict for so long, on Wilmslow Road.

Fairfield and Brooklands

St Hilary's, Alderley Edge, Hurst Lea.

Hurst Lea

Large unattractive yellow brick Italianate villa. Here lived Jacob Bright MP *".... Ursula's husband, and John's brother, but more of the former than the latter"* quotes *'Manchester Faces and Places'* Vol 1, unkindly.

It was bought by St Hilary's 1920 as the headmistress' house and boarding house. The girls walked up and down through the village, daily, in a blue crocodile. Hurst Lea was sold in 1963 after the purchase of Barnfield, and demolished. Flats occupy the site today.

MR. JACOB BRIGHT, M.P.
(From a Photograph by Franz Baum.)

On Ryley's Lane is ....

The Meadows

Attractive smooth white Regency-style villa. It seems to face the wrong way, with the untidy offices to the road and the symmetrical front to the garden. This can be explained .....

On 29 September 1847 the first Indenture was made between Thomas Joseph de Trafford and Richard Martin Esq of Manchester, Drysalter, for a parcel of land with a covenant to build and finish a house or houses on it within two years. The minimum quality of the house(s) is minutely specified, as is what can NOT be built. The land was leased for 999 years at an annual payment of £35 7s 6d. The de Traffords retained mineral rights. All this was standard de Trafford stuff, so we can presume that The Meadows was built and finished by 29 Sept 1849.

The original parcel was in fact divided into two, unequally. **Burnside** was built on the larger portion, presumably also by Richard Martin, and leased or sold to George Tunstall Redmayne, architect, partner and brother-in-law to Alfred Waterhouse. It was bought by the sisters of St Joseph in 1942, who were soon to start Mount Carmel school, and demolished some years later. In 1852 Richard Martin acquired a further triangular parcel of land across the road with the same two-year covenant, so we can presume that the large semis there,

Brookside Villas, were built and finished by the end of 1854. The map accompanying the deeds shows that the de Traffords allowed for a new road at the back, where the park is now. This is why The Meadows was built the wrong way round.

The house as first built was quite modest: two handsome living rooms facing south, with shallow curved bows, and the intended entrance hall in between leading to a central stair and side entrance. Kitchen and pantry to Ryley's Lane. Cellars. Yard, pump, small range of outbuildings at the side. Upstairs two fine bedrooms and two smaller ones. A minute stair to a single attic. Long garden with a cedar, probably of 1848. Total parcel 2,758 square yards with an annual rent of £11 19s 10d (1886 and now) to be paid to the holders of Burnside.

In 1886 it was bought by Mountford Spencer of Heaton Moor, machine maker, for £2,243. He added a new wing, which upset the symmetry, with a polygonal bow on each floor, making a new dining room below and master bedroom above. Executed in yellow brick painted white, and in a more Victorian style. The bathroom was extended and a WC added at the same time.

In 1908 another extension was made on the northwest corner to make a new entrance hall and a WC downstairs and two bedrooms upstairs. Isaac Massey & Son were the builders. The extension is carefully blended in with the original villa, e.g. see the string course, unlike the 1886 extension. It looks as though the original front door and its surround were re-used - Massey's were good at that sort of thing. Inside though the details are typical of its date.

From 1924 to 1945 it was the home of Philip Godlee, who was an interesting enough man to have a book written about him, 'Philip Godlee by His Friends' 1954. He was a member of a group of inter-related families, the Haworths and the Gaddums, whose lives are recorded in privately printed books. Philip Godlee travelled daily on the 8.32am train, in company with Hubert Worthington, Arthur Broadhurst, Dr Heywood and others, on his way to the weaving mill, Simpson and Godlee Limited. He had been badly injured by a Mills bomb in the first world war and had to undergo a series of operations on his leg. The book recalls the high jinks on the train after one such absence, when he was welcomed back to the 'carriage' with a red carpet, potted palms and appropriate music. Perhaps his chief claim to fame was when he took over the chairmanship of the Hallé in 1942. The fortunes of the orchestra were at their lowest. In the teeth of committee opposition he made the players fully professional for the first time and invited over a young conductor from New York called John Barbirolli.

134

The unimpressive frontage of The Meadows on Ryley's Lane.

Not often photographed are the miscellaneous, but essential, outhouses and yard of a villa.

The garden side of the Meadows is very much finer.

A beaten copper firescreen at The Meadows, made by James Smithies of Wilmslow. Mr Smithies' work is common in the area.

Far right: the front door, uncomfortably sited at the side of the house.

Interior view of one of th elegant Regency-style bays of The Meadows.

Another view of the yard shows a large pen for a hound, and the old pump being slowly eaten by an Ash tree.

· THE · MEADOWS · ALDERLEY · EDGE · CHESHIRE ·

· Scale · 8 · Feet · to · the · Inch ·

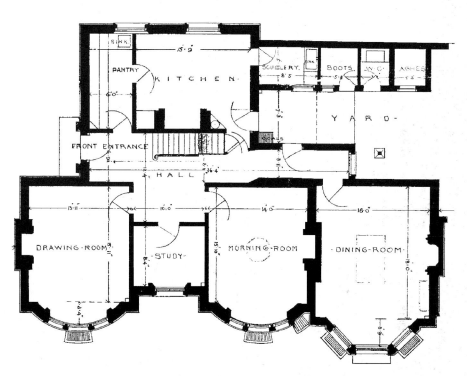

· Ground · Floor · Plan ·

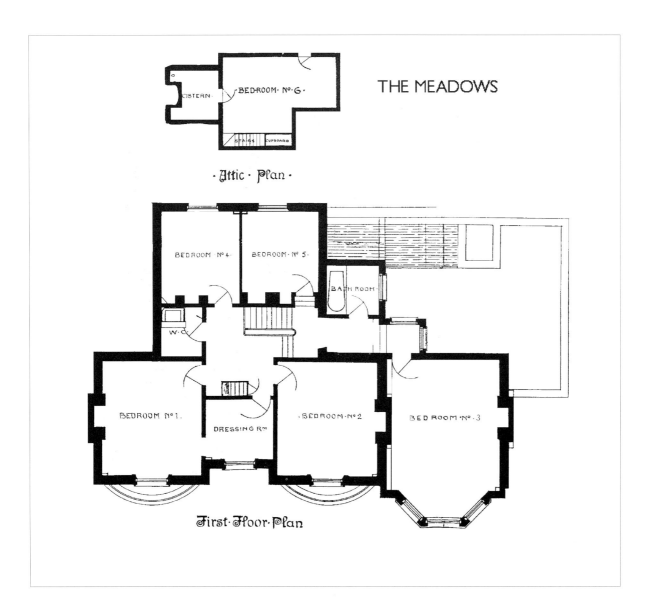

THE MEADOWS

·Attic· Plan·

First·Floor·Plan

139

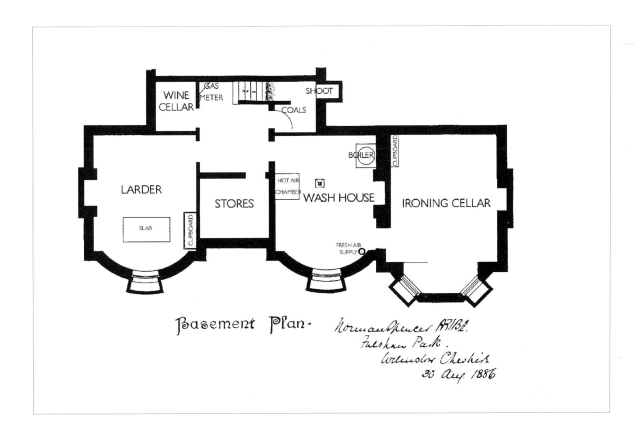

Basement Plan.

140

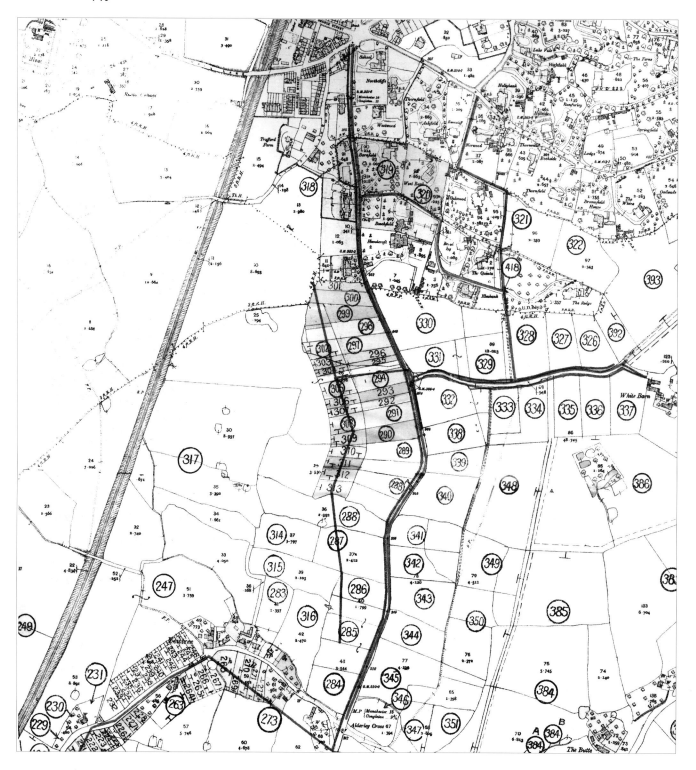

A SHORT GAZETTEER OF THE SECOND GENERATION OF VILLAS

At the top of Macclesfield Road are .....

Abbot Brow

Built by Massey's for E L Heyworth and one of their best. Designed by Hubert Worthington. There is an oval plaque above the middle window of the south front with the Heyworth initials, exactly as at Penn. The Agnews extended the house in 1933 by adding a nursery wing on the west end, also by Massey's and Hubert Worthington. This is now a separate dwelling.

Next came Raymond King and his brother Arthur, carpet manufacturers of Collyhurst. They moved the business to Northern Ireland but then lost their main customer, which was the Railway.

The house was considered to be worth an article in the 'Architectural Review' in 1924. As first built it was symmetrical; a central block with a high hipped roof and dormers, flanked by two single-storey wings with flat roofs. The 1933 extension replaced the low garage wing. An extra dormer was put in at the back, which helps to ease the transition from symmetry to asymmetry. The effect on the massing and overall appearance of the house is probably an improvement.

The house is very imposing from a distance, because of big enfolding roof and very tall unadorned chimneys, and the ambitious formula of five bays with wings. Closer at hand the illusion of a large house is given by the smaller-than-usual bricks, each one outlined in white pointing. After this, the big surprise is the remarkably modest interior. The house is the opposite of the 'Tardis', much smaller inside than outside. It is interesting that the *'Architectural Review'* includes criticism on the grounds of deceitfulness.

The planning is simple. A row of living rooms downstairs and bedrooms upstairs faces south over the garden, and the north side is taken with circulation and pantries, bathrooms, etc. All the rooms are small, low-ceilinged and simply articulated. It is interesting that a maid's sitting room, butler's pantry and maid's bedroom and bathroom are still included at this late date and in quite a modest house.

The quality throughout is A1. When Massey's were working on the house on later occasions they apparently brought their apprentices up to see the joinery of the roof, on the grounds that they would never see better. Very pleasant, light, and manageable bringing to mind the phrase "sweetness and light" used by Mark Girouard as the title for his book on 'Queen Anne' architecture.

Good garden; the front has been sold off for building but the rear looks out over fields which were bought jointly by the residents and then presented to the National Trust to prevent development.

Abbot Brow
Front enrance

Edgecroft

The topmost house on the Edge except for Armstrong farm, it was built in 1907 or 1908 for Emily Powell of Wilmslow and her husband James Henry Powell, merchant at W. Hardcastle & Co, 27 Sackville St Manchester. They stayed thirty years and so have each of the two subsequent owners. The land was leased for £700, followed by a yearly rent of a peppercorn, rather than the usual steady annual rents.

Not an immediately attractive house, lacking the discipline of Abbot Brow next door, although it is on a magnificent site. It was altered in the 1930s and again very extensively in the 1960s when the whole back elevation was rebuilt with picture windows and flat roofs. Hard brick, pebbledash, a bit of red sandstone ashlar round the door, timber-framed gables with carved but not shaped bargeboards. Shell hood over front door, curved out centre pane in one upstairs window, i.e. very dilute Norman Shaw. Red tile roof.

The interior is unconventionally planned and detailed, clearly to the clients' specifications. There are hidden built-in safes, and the coal hods for the fireplaces are hidden in special recesses in the panelling. Spacious reception hall with the staircase rising out of it in a big angled window at the front. Upstairs a long corridor running parallel to the front of the house lined with walk-in linen cupboards. Six bedrooms, three bathrooms. The bathrooms were all done up 60s style, with endlessly repeating mirrors; one lilac, one spearmint and one bacterial green. The servants quarters have been altered, doing away with any back stair, but the butler's pantry and big kitchen are still recognisable.

The present owners have returned it all as far as possible to its original state, reversing the 60s work, with shallow curved 'Bayko' bays - for those who remember that excellent toy. The architect, Edward Hiley of Manchester, found that when he came to measure up it all fitted together remarkably well, with neat figures and proportions. Likewise the builders say it is all square and shipshape. A typical Alderley Edge job in fact.

The stable block, linked to house by a glazed roof, is of interest because little altered. Carriage house, workshop, loose boxes below with a hayloft above, and a small dwelling for the coachman at the back, consisting of little kitchen with sink and range downstairs and two rooms upstairs. A previous owner lived here for a while, so I am told, when chucked out by his wife. Potting sheds and boilerhouse converted to a sauna and plunge pool. Foundation of big double greenhouse visible. The gardens, reduced from the original $1\frac{3}{4}$ acres, are rather bleak, although there are some big conifers in front. Nice gatepiers with big round stone balls on top. One of them was once knocked off, started to roll down the hill, but fell into a hole in the road - Phew! Luckily no-one was in the hole, it being teabreak time.

Greylands

Called Greystead on 1909 map, not there 1898. Shallow tiled roof somewhat Swiss style at end. Battered chimneys. Wooden casements. White roughcast. Stands on a terrace with unshaped stone balustrade. Good Alderley Edge drive through rocks and shrubbery.

Front Elevation

Penn

Dated 1912 on an oval plaque above the garden door with the entwined initials WDM - Walter and Dorothy Milne. White rendered neo-Georgian house with sash windows throughout. Sprocketed eaved roof in graded Lake District slate. Symmetrical seven bay centre, with two round bows with curved glass on the right-hand end, and a lower wing running back at right angles on the left; both added to the main block in an oddly inorganic fashion. Also a wooden garden room in front of the crosswing, looking like an afterthought but on the original plan. Visitors to the famous gardens perceived this as the front of the house, but the other side, where the drive goes, reveals the front door under a flat hood. To one side of the courtyard is the crosswing, with door under two round arches. The roof of the main block on this side is very complicated, with three hipped gables coming forwards.

The architect of Penn was Percy Worthington. He was 22 years older than his half-brother Hubert. It is easy to see that Penn and Abbott Brow come from the same firm, and also easy to see that each is the work a different brother; the two houses give very much the same impression of assured craftsmanship in a classical mode, but when analysed are found to differ in almost every particular.

Penn's garden has been very well known and regularly open to the public. Bowl of grass with choice rhododendrons around under large trees including an old cedar and a further rocky area with narrow paths and many more rhododendrons.

The garage by the Woodbrook Road gate marks the site of an old timber-framed cottage, called **Mountain of Poverty**, home of the Ridgeways, who were said to be 'poorer than the land itself'.

Walter and Dorothy Milne also built Dawstone at Windermere by Dan Gibson.

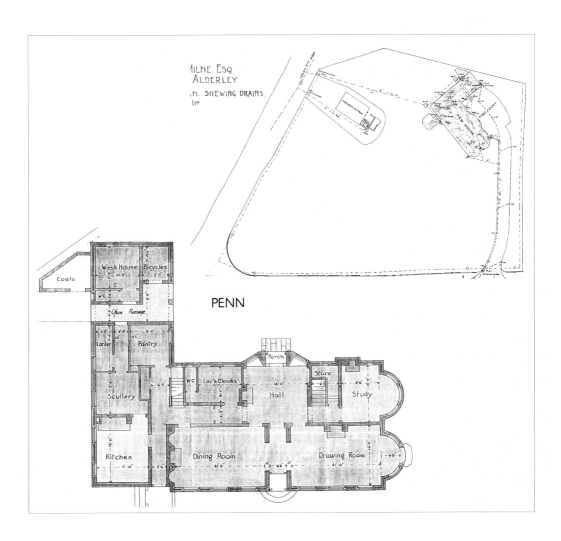

On Congleton Road and Whitebarn Road .....

Only a very small selection is listed here. Strictly speaking these are not in Alderley Edge at all, but in Alderley. They fall in St Mary's Parish, not St Philip's, and they trail away into the countryside. I have therefore chosen just a few, all at the Alderley Edge end.

Greythwaite, otherwise 34 Congleton Road

Dated 1909 on a rainwater hopper; by Harry Fairhurst, built by Isaac Massey & Sons for Mrs Schute. Original plans extant. A white roughcast house, perhaps a little ungainly but with an interesting plan featuring canted walls. A section of timber-framing is displayed in the front gable almost as 'shed-plus-sign' saying *"this is a Cheshire cottage"*.

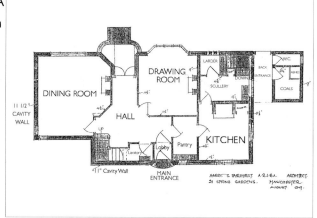

Plan and garden front of Greythwaite; contrast p 45.
   Courtesy Nick and Julie Clayton

EAST-ELEVATION

Hill Cottage, Congleton Road

Pair of semis with **Sandhurst.** 1910 by A Edgar Beresford for T O Bridge and built by Massey's. Beresford was the partner of Baillie Scott, now renowned as one if the best of the Arts-and-Crafts architects. He was also Mrs Bridge's brother, originally from Macclesfield.

Beresford's plans, his typewritten specifications, Massey's accounts all in best copperplate handwriting and correct to the nearest ha'penny, and Baillie Scott and Beresford's beautiful book *"Homes and Gardens"* are all preserved there. The Bridges moved from Trafford Road to their new house in 1911, together with a single maid, Minnie. Mr and Mrs Bridge's son Geoffrey, who was three when they moved, only sold Hill Cottage in July 1998 so he was there, with one short interval, for 87 years.

Even now the house is little changed, and very charming it is too. Although modest compared with the Victorian villas, it is cleverly designed to catch the sun and the view. The interior is made to seem more spacious than it really is by the use of a folding partition between the living rooms - a typical Baillie Scott touch this - and a glazed oak screen to the entrance hall. Some of the fireplaces are almost worthy of Mackintosh and the craftsmanship is excellent throughout.

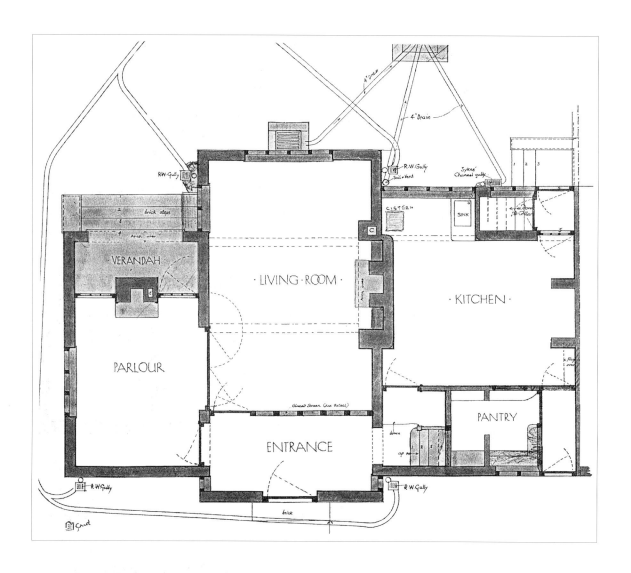

VERANDAH

LIVING·ROOM

KITCHEN

PARLOUR

ENTRANCE

PANTRY

CISTERN

SINK

R.W.Gully

R.W.Gully

Soil & Vent

Sykes' Channel gully

brick steps

Arch over

4" Drain

4" Drain

Glazed Screen (see detail)

brick

R.W.Gully

R.W.Gully

down

cup

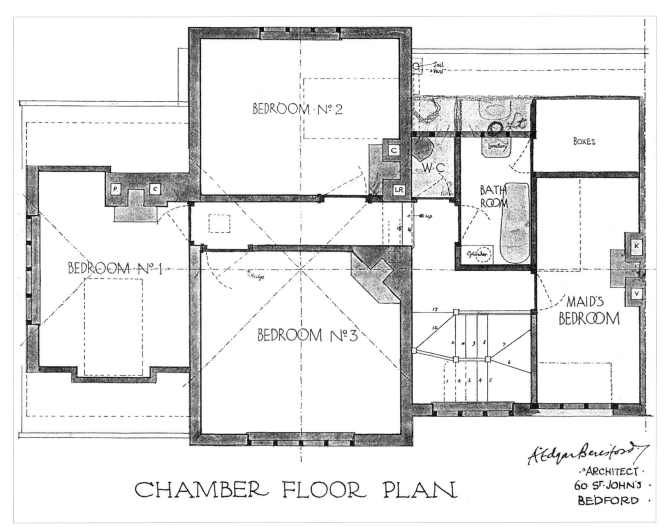

CHAMBER FLOOR PLAN

A Edgar Beresford
·ARCHITECT·
60 St·JOHN'S·
BEDFORD·

WEST ELEVATION

Plans of Hill Cottage. Note the glazed screen and the folding doors of the living room which allow the internal space to flow, and the way the parlour is opened up to the verandah and garden.

Courtesy Roger & Elaine Williams

Longmynd, Congleton Road

For A V Sugden Esq., Messrs Halliday and Agate architects, who also built the Festival Hall, and built by Massey's. Very large house, many-gabled. White roughcast with a stone roof. Tennis court with special loggia.

Pantiles, originally called **Strathyre**, **Congleton Road**

A Lutyensish house designed by F Milton Cashmore, whose plans are extant, and built by Massey's. One of a pair of semis, with a second pair next door to the same plan but different detail. Land was leased for building in 1910 but, delayed by the war, the houses were not built until 1919-20. Even then they had to be bought in by the firm, and then rented before being finally sold.

The buyer in 1928 was Miss Joan Banham, soon to become the wife of Hubert Worthington. It was her home for more than 50 years. Hubert designed the garage extension, and the fireplace and shelving in the living room. Eric Gill stayed when working at the cathedral. When Sir Hubert died Lady W divided the house, putting in a second stair etc to her own design, but it is now back as one.

A deep L-shaped house so that the pair makes a U, with the front door in the angle. Quite a complex plan. This pair has pantiled roof of course, with wood and lead gutters, white casements with flat leads over the dormers, yellow roughcast. The other pair has flat tiles with pitches over the dormers, standard iron guttering, exposed red brick and simpler glazing to the windows.

Silver Trees, White Barn Road

By P G (Gary) Fairhurst, the second one of the dynasty. Not on Massey's list. Harry Fairhurst recalls, as a boy, learning to lay floorboards here, in the maid's room.

Tan-y-Rallt, White Barn Road

1924. Designed by P G Fairhurst for himself, in the firm's name Harry S Fairhurst. He built himself a seaside house called **Sea Garth** at the same time, at Red Wharf Bay in Anglesey. He was twenty-three or -four at the time and just qualified. The site was found by accident - he and his fiancee were attending a dinner party at White Barn House when they learned that the plot next door was for sale. Building work was delayed by a strike, only finished in 1925. Here was born 1925 Harry Fairhurst, the third architect of the dynasty.
It's a red brick house with a curved stair turret; recently altered.

Whitebarn Lodge

1925 for Mr. Donald; one of three designed by Henry Boddington of London and built by Massey's. Each house had to have a site of at least one acre. Henry Boddington was the grandson of the founder of the famous Strangeways brewery. His father, Henry II, turned **Pownall Hall,** Wilmslow, into a very advanced artistic house. Whitebarn Lodge is a big artsy craftsy house, long and low, in white pebbledash, with a stone roof.

White Barn Cottage

1913 for T Crompton Peatfield Esq. Isaac Massey builder
Variegated flat-tile roof, red brick chimneys, white Queen Anne type windows, cream-painted pebbledash render, pretty big. The ICI/Zeneca hospitality house, complete with butler, following demolition of the Ridge.

One of three blocks of Gardener's Houses in Orchard Green, designed by Hubert Worthington in 1920.

The White House, Congleton Road

The first one past the de Trafford/Stanley boundary. Massey lists '*1910 garage and dwelling-house for T Eadington, W M Gillow Esq architect'*. Note Mr Eadington does not merit the designation Esq; he was a cycle maker and dealer.

White roughcast house with Voyseyish details such as flat stone mullioned windows and a bottleglass window above front door. Prominent built-in shelter by the front door, probably for a bicycle. At the back a verandah and a Stanley gable. It is a big house despite the cottagey look. There are original electrics with big beaten copper switches, and the house incorporates salvaged items from demolitions and alterations carried out by the firm elsewhere - the front door from Wooton Hall near Ashbourne, the glass roundels from Portal at Tarporley, old beams from a house at Henbury. In 1924 Massey's built Mr Eadington a showroom, lockup and garage in London Road. It was recently turned into a cafe bar, the first of many I dare say.

Windy Howe, Whitebarn Road

1909 by F W Mee for Harold King Esq. Isaac Massey builder. A large house. Variegated flat-tile roof. Long elevation to the south with balcony over a columned porch, triple gables to the west with oriels rather like Edgecroft. Pebbledash render painted cream, white paintwork.

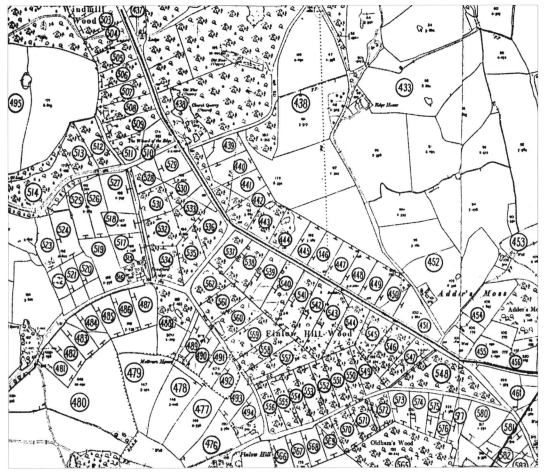

THE STANLEY SALE CATALOGUE 1938

The following few pages are intended to give a sample of the 661 lots of Stanley sale. It was as great a milestone, in its way, in the history of the Edge as the coming of the railway, marking as it did the complete divorce of the family from the place it had identified with for so long.

The map above and some of the lots that follow indicate the way that the estate was carved up into villa plots for the sale. If it had gone ahead as planned there would be very little of Alderley Edge to be enjoyed today, except in little plots fenced off as private gardens.

The catalogue itself is an invaluable document for the study of the Stanley Estate at Alderley, but of course it makes no reference to the neighbouring De Trafford estate where all the first villa development took place. The later villas are all here, listed as Freehold Ground Rents, but the agents did not see fit to illustrate any of them.

LOT 434 (*Withdrawn*)
(Coloured Brown on Plan No. 2).

The Clockhouse and Part Waterfall Woods

containing about

17a. 2r. 35p.

being O.S. No. 37 (17.401 acres) and O.S. No. 38 (.322 acre) in the Parish of Over Alderley adjoining the Clockhouse and Edge House Farms.

Now in hand.

Timber has been valued at £550, and is included in Sale.

See Lot 432 as ᵂ water pipe and also as to Right-of-Way.

LOT 435 (*Withdrawn*)
(Coloured Green on Plan No. 2).

The Dicken's Wood

containing about

24a. 3r. 24p.

being O.S. No. 45 (21.595 acres) and O.S. No. 46 (3.307 acres) in the Parish of Over Alderley.

Access to this Lot over road O.S. No. 173.

Now in hand.

Timber valued at £625 is included in the Sale.

LOT 436 (*Withdrawn*)
(Coloured Orange on Plan No. 2).

The Wizard Woods

situated on a high promontory known as Alderley Edge commanding views across the Cheshire Plains to the Hills of Wales, containing about

41 Acres

An exceptionally Attractive and Valuable Building Estate with frontages to the Macclesfield Road and the Edge House Lane.

All Services are available.

The Timber on this Lot is held in trust by the Alderley Edge U.D.C. on behalf of the Council for the Preservation of Rural England.

Included in this Lot is the well known CASTLE ROCK.

SCHEDULE.

No. on Plan.	Description.				Acreage.
Pt. 162	Wizard Wood ...	...	...	...	19.000
Pt. 166	Ditto ...	...	...	...	20.521
177	The Engine Vein Mine	...	...	.426
173	Track ...	...	...	...	.986
				A.	40.933

LOT 437
(Coloured Blue on Plan No. 2).

An Attractive Cottage

known as

The Beacon Lodge

built of red sandstone and of pleasing elevation, containing Kitchen, Scullery, etc., and Two Bed Rooms, having a **good garden**, within 1 mile of Alderley Edge Station, being Part O.S. No. 162 (.582 acre).

Let on a Monthly Tenancy at a yearly rent of £8 0s. 0d. to Mr. J. W. Norbury.

LOT 438 (*Part Withdrawn*)
(Coloured Pink on Plan No. 2).

The Well-known and Picturesque Premises

known as

The Wizard of the Edge

Used as a Café and Dairy Farm

situated in a commanding position on the main Alderley Edge-Macclesfield Road.

In area about

26a. 2r. 29p.

The premises include Temperance Hotel, built of brick with a tiled roof, and containing the usual Kitchen offices, Two Tea Rooms, Old Bar and Five Bed Rooms.

The Outbuildings

include Wash-house, Nine-Tie Shippon, Barn with loft over, Nine-Tie Shippon with fodder bing, Two-Stall Stable, Piggeries, Two-Bay Cart ,Shed and large old building.

Water from Well and Main Water available.

SCHEDULE.

No. on Plan.	Description.				Acreage.
176	House and Buildings	...	...	.803
Pt. 166	Woods in hand	...	...	...	.500
180	Woods (in hand)	...	...	...	1.343
Pt. 179	Arable	...	...	...	...	4.638
181	Ditto	...	...	...	...	3.517
Pt. 182	Ditto	...	...	...	...	.992
165	Ditto	...	...	...	...	4.032
47	Arable	...	...	...	...	1.358
48	Wooden Hut	...	...	...	1.503
97	Arable	...	...	...	...	1.344
Pt. 99	Ditto	...	...	...	...	3.250
				A.	23.280

Let to Mr. F. Wright on Annual Tenancy at an Apportioned Rent of £50.

Wood O.S. No. 180 and Parts O.S. No. 16, in hand.

Wooden hut site let to Mr. R. L. Hidderley at £1 a year.

Apportioned Tithe: Timber: £106.

Lot 431.   Clockhouse Farm.

Lot 437.   Beacon Lodge.

Lot 500.   Cottage at Copper Mines.

Lot 438.   Wizard Cafe.

The Outbuildings

include a Loose Box, Barn, Four-Tie Shippon with loft over all.

SCHEDULE.

No. on Plan.	Description.				Acreage.
298	House and Buildings	...	...	...	.270
319	Arable	...	...	...	1.376
Pt. 318	Pasture	...	...	...	1.069
				A.	2.715

Part let on Annual Tenancy to Mr. R. L. Thompson at a rent of £8 10s. 0d., and Part O.S. No. 318 let with other lands to Mr. C. Potts on an Annual Tenancy at an Apportioned Rent of £2 4s. 0d.

Apportioned Tithe:

LOT 579
(Coloured Pink on Plan No. 2).

A pleasantly situated potential

Building Site

adjoining Sycamore Farm and having a frontage to Slade Lane of about 320 feet.

In area about

2a.   1r.   28p.

Being O.S. No. 297 (2.428 acres).

Electricity and water nearby.

Let, with other land, to Mr. J. R. Downes on Annual Tenancy at an Apportioned Rent of £6 5s. 0d.

Apportioned Tithe:

LOT 580
(Coloured Brown on Plan No. 2).

An Attractive

Building Site

in area about

1a.   3r.   3p.

Situated at the junction of Finlow Hill Lane and the main Macclesfield Road and having a frontage of 300 feet to the former.

Being O.S. No. 317 (1.771 acres).

Electricity and water nearby.

Let, with other lands, to Mr. Clement Potts on Annual Tenancy at an Apportioned Rent of £3 13s. 0d.

Apportioned Tithe:

LOT 581
(Coloured Blue on Plan No. 2).

A Valuable

Building Plot

4,350 sq. yds. Part O.S. Nos. 316 and 318 (.901 acre).

Situated on the main Macclesfield Road and having a frontage thereto of about 130 feet and a depth of 300 feet.

Services. Company's Water and Electricity nearby.

Let, with other lands, to Mr. Clement Potts, on Annual Tenancy at an Apportioned Rent of £1 17s. 0d.

Apportioned Tithe:

LOT 582
(Coloured Pink on Plan No. 2).

A Similar Plot

4,700 sq. yds. with a frontage of about 150 feet and a depth of about 300 feet.

Let as above at an Apportioned Rent of £2 1s. 0d.

Apportioned Tithe:

LOT 583
(Coloured Yellow on Plan No. 2).

A Valuable

Corner Building Plot

Adjoining the previous Lot. Being Part O.S. Nos. 316 and 318 (.654 acre), having nearly 150 feet of frontage to the Main Alderley Macclesfield Road and a return of nearly 200 feet to Slade Green Lane.

The whole
in area about 3,150 sq. yds.

Electricity on Plot and water nearby.

Let, with other lands, to Mr. Clement Potts on Annual Tenancy at an Apportioned Rent of £1 7s. 0d.

Apportioned Tithe:

LOT 584
(Coloured Blue on Plan No. 2).

A Very Desirable Mixed and Dairy Farm
known as
"Higher House Farm"
Hocker Lane, Over Alderley,
in area about

71a.   2r.   24p.

The House

is brick built with a stone and slated roof, and the accommodation includes Dining Room, Living Kitchen with tiled floor, Buttery with slated shelves, Tiled Dairy, Press-room and Larder, while on the first floor there are Five Bed Rooms and Four Bed Rooms above.

The Outbuildings

include Loose Box, Six-Tie Shippon with fodder bing and Loft over, Four-Bay covered Barn, Bull Box and Calf Shed, Five-Tie Shippon, Two Ten-Tie Shippons with fodder bing between, Meal House, Three-Stall Stable and Three Piggeries.

SCHEDULE.

No. on Plan.	Description.				Acreage.
176	House and Buildings	...	...	...	1.303
171	Arable	...	...	...	15.046
171a	Ditto	...	...	...	8.180
182	Pasture	...	...	...	13.206
181	Part, Arable, Part Pasture	...	...	9.902
177	Pasture	...	...	...	2.048
141	Ditto	...	...	...	11.515
175	Ditto	...	...	...	5.809
170	Wood (in hand)	...	...	...	4.342
173	Wood (in hand)	...	...	...	.300
				A.	71.651

Let on Annual Tenancy to Mr. G. Oakes at a rent of £134.

The Reservoir and pipes in O.S. No. 175 and rights of access thereto are reserved (see Lot 126a).

Tithe:

Timber: £310.

Lot 584.   Higher House Farm.

Lot 585.   Acton Farm.

Lot 586.   Baguley Farm.

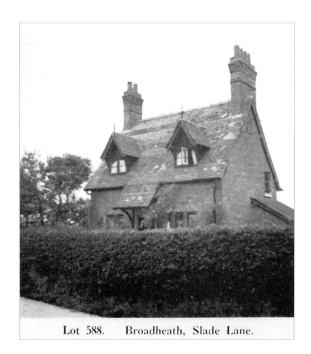

Lot 588.   Broadheath, Slade Lane.

158

LOT 292
(Coloured Brown on Plan No. 1).

A WELL-SECURED

Freehold Ground Rent

on premises at Alderley Edge known as "Hill Cottage," Congleton Road, held by Mr. T. O. Bridge, on lease for 999 years from 24th June, 1910, at a Ground Rent of £8 13s. 6d. per annum.

LOT 293
(Coloured Green on Plan No. 1).

ANOTHER WELL-SECURED

Freehold Ground Rent

on premises at Alderley Edge, known as "Sandhurst," held by executors of S. I. Massey, on lease for 999 years from 24th June, 1910, at a Ground Rent of £9 4s. 8d. per annum.

LOT 294
(Coloured Pink on Plan No. 1).

ANOTHER WELL-SECURED

Freehold Ground Rent

on premises at Alderley Edge, known as "Langdale," held by Mrs. Constance Forrester on lease for 999 years from 25th December, 1910, at a Ground Rent of £12 10s. 4d. per annum.

LOT 295
(Coloured Blue on Plan No. 1).

A WELL-SECURED

Freehold Ground Rent

on premises at Alderley Edge known as "Pantiles," held by Mrs. H. Worthington on lease jointly with Lot 296, for 999 years from 25th December, 1910, at a Ground Rent of £6 5s. 2d. per annum (part of total Ground Rent of £12 13s. 2d.).

LOT 296
(Coloured Blue on Plan No. 1).

A WELL-SECURED

Freehold Ground Rent

on premises at Alderley Edge, known as Brag Cottage, held by Mr. James Porter on lease jointly with Lot 295 for 999 years from 25th December, 1910, at a Ground Rent of £6 8s. 0d. per annum (part of total Ground Rent of £12 13s. 2d.).

LOT 297
(Coloured Pink on Plan No. 1).

A WELL-SECURED

Freehold Ground Rent

on premises at Alderley, known as "Cranford," held by Mr. H. Padfield on lease for 999 years from 25th March, 1909, at a Ground Rent of £14 13s. 0d. per annum.

LOT 298
(Coloured Yellow on Plan No. 1).

A SIMILARLY WELL-SECURED

Ground Rent

on premises at Alderley Edge, known as "Lyneal," held by Mrs. A. B. Ward on lease for 999 years from 25th March, 1909, at a Ground Rent of £19 per annum.

LOT 299
(Coloured Green on Plan No. 1).

ANOTHER WELL-SECURED

Freehold Ground Rent

on premises at Alderley Edge, known as "Netherly," held by Mr. H. Frost on lease for 999 years from 25th December, 1908, at a Ground Rent of £14 11s. 10d. per annum.

LOT 300
(Coloured Blue on Plan No. 1).

ANOTHER WELL-SECURED

Freehold Ground Rent

on premises at Alderley Edge, known as "White House," held by Mr. Geoffrey Senior, on lease for 999 years from 25th December, 1908, at a Ground Rent of £12 13s. 8d. per annum.

LOT 301
(Coloured Pink on Plan No. 1).

Plot of Land

subject to a lease for 999 years from 24th June, 1908, at Congleton Road, Alderley Edge, held by Mr. W. H. Welsh at a Peppercorn Rent. Lease prohibits land to be built on.

LOT 302
(Coloured Brown on Plan No. 1).

A Small Parcel of Desirable

Building Land

at rear of Lot 297, containing about 2,400 sq. yds., being Part O S. No. 26 (.495 acre).

Let with other land to Mr. G. Worthington on Annual Tenancy at an Apportioned Rent of 8s.

Apportioned Tithe:

LOT 303
(Coloured Blue on Plan No. 1).

A Similar Plot

at rear of Lot 296, containing about 1,150 sq. yds., being Part O.S. No. 26 (.240 acre).

Let as above at an Apportioned Rent of 3s.

Dickens Wood, Clockhouse Wood and Wizard Woods, lots 434, 435 and 436, formed part of the gift made by the Pilkington sisters of Firwood to the National Trust, and hence to us all.

the Silk Press

the Publishing House for Cheshire,
the Moorlands and the Peak

Other titles available include:

'A Sketch of the Parish of Prestbury' by George Yamold Osborne
Hard cover, with new illustrations. 750 numbered copies £23 (Presentation edition in slip case £28.50)

'Swythamley and its Neighbourhood' by Sir Philip Brocklehurst
Hard cover with illustrations from original photographs 500 numbered copies £18.95

'Scientific Rambles Round Macclesfield'
by J D Sainter, with an introduction by Alan Garner Hard cover, newly illustrated. 750 numbered copies £18.95

'Views in the High Peaks of Derbyshire' with an introduction by Mike Langham
Lavishly illustrated, top quality soft cover £5.95

In preparation:

Our special millenium edition of
Yates' **'History of Congleton'** Due Spring 2000 Price TBA

These titles may be ordered direct from the Publishers at.

The Silk Press, Grosvenor House
45 The Downs, Altrincham, Cheshire WA14 2QG
Telephone: 0161 929 4884 or 0161 928 0333
Fax: 070707 39898

Please enclose payment as listed, adding £2.50 for postage and packing and an extra 75p per volume for multiple orders.